POWER OF WILL

Frank Channing Haddock (17 November 1853–9 February 1915) was a renowned New Thought and self-help author, known for his teachings on philosophy, ethics, spirituality, cultivation of the will and empowerment. He graduated from St Lawrence University in 1876. Haddock later entered the Methodist ministry, but left it to take up law. He practised in Milwaukee, Wisconsin and was a renowned legal writer. In 1887, he returned to the ministry, preaching in Iowa, Ohio and Massachusetts. After retiring from the ministry, he resumed writing.

Some of his well-known works include *Power for Success*, *The Personal Atmosphere*, *Business Power*, *The Culture of Courage*, *Practical Psychology* and *Creative Personality*.

POWER OF WILL

A PRACTICAL BOOK FOR UNFOLDING THE POWERS OF MIND

FRANK CHANNING HADDOCK

RUPA

Published by
Rupa Publications India Pvt. Ltd 2019
7/16, Ansari Road, Daryaganj
New Delhi 110002

Sales centres:
Allahabad Bengaluru Chennai
Hyderabad Jaipur Kathmandu
Kolkata Mumbai

ISBN: 978-93-5333-703-2

First impression 2019

10 9 8 7 6 5 4 3 2 1

CONTENTS

PART IV
DESTRUCTION OF HABIT

PREFACE

This book comes to you as a Well-wisher, a Teacher, and a Prophet. It will become a Teacher if you will honestly try to secure mental reaction upon it; that is, if you will resolve to THINK—to Think *with* it and to Think *into* it.

It will be Prophet of a higher and more successful living if you will persistently and intelligently follow its requirements, for this will make yourself a completer Manual of the Perfected Will.

But remember! This book cannot think for you. THAT IS THE TASK OF YOUR MIND.

This book cannot give you greater power of Will. THAT IS FOR YOU TO ACQUIRE BY THE RIGHT USE OF ITS CONTENTS.

This book cannot hold you to persistence in self-culture. THAT IS THE TEST OF YOUR WILL.

This book is not magical. It promises nothing occult or mysterious. It is simply a call to practical and scientific work.

If you will steadfastly go on through the requirements marked out in this book, it will help develop within you the highest wishes of welfare for self. It will make you a teacher of self. It will inspire you as a prophet of self brought to largest efficiency.

All now rests with you!

PART I

THE WILL AND SUCCESS

CHAPTER I

THE WILL AND ITS ACTION

There has been altogether too much talk about the secret of success. Success has no secret. Her voice is forever ringing through the marketplace and crying in the wilderness, and the burden of her cry is one word—will. Any normal young man [person] who hears and heeds that cry is equipped fully to climb to the very heights of life. If there is one thing I have tried to do through these years, it is to indent in the minds of the men of America the living fact that when they give Will the reins and say 'Drive!' they are headed toward the heights.

—Dr Russell H. Conwell

The human Will involves mysteries that have never been fathomed. As a "faculty" of the mind, it is, nevertheless, a familiar and practical reality. There are those who deny man's spiritual nature, but no one calls in question the existence of this power. While differences obtain among writers as to its source, its constitution, its functions, its limitations, its freedom, all concede that the Will itself is an actual part of the mind of man, and that its place and uses in our life are of transcendent importance.

Disagreements as to its interpretations do not destroy these facts.

The Will is sometimes defined as the "faculty of conscious, and especially of deliberative action". Whether the word "conscious" is essential to the definition may be questioned. Some actions that are unconscious are, nevertheless, probably expressions of the Will; and some involuntary acts are certainly conscious. All voluntary acts are deliberative, for deliberation may proceed "with the swiftness of lightning", as the saying goes, but both deliberation and its attendant actions are not always conscious. A better definition of the word "Will", therefore, is "THE POWER OF SELF-DIRECTION".

This power acts in conjunction with *feeling* and *knowledge,* but is not to be identified with them as a matter of definition. Nor ought it to be confounded with *desire,* nor with the *moral sense.* One may feel without willing, and one may will contrary to feeling. So the Will may proceed either with knowledge or in opposition thereto, or, indeed, in a manner indifferent. Oftentimes, desires are experienced that are unaccompanied by acts of Will, and the moral sense frequently becomes the sole occasion of willing, or it is set aside by the Will, whatever the ethical dictates in the case.

Present Definitions

The Will is a way a person has of being and doing, by which itself and the body in which it dwells are directed.

It is not the Will that wills, any more than it is the perceptive powers that perceive, or the faculty of imagination that pictures mental images.

The Will is "the Soul Itself Exercising Self-direction".

"By the term 'Will' in the narrower sense," says Royce, "one very commonly means so much of our mental life as involves the *attentive guidance of our conduct.*"

When a person employs this instrumental power, it puts forth a *Volition.*

A Volition is the willing power in action.

All Volitions are thus *secondary mental commands* for appropriate mental or physical acts.

Obedience of mind or body to Volitions *exhibits the power* of the Will.

No one wills the impossible for himself. One cannot will to raise a paralyzed arm, nor to fly in the air without any machinery.

In such cases, there may be the desire to act, but the mind refuses to will—that is, to put forth a Volition, which is a secondary command—when obedience, of the mind itself, or of the body, is known to lie beyond the range of the possible.

The Will may be regarded as both *Static* and *Dynamic.*

In one case, it is a *power of person* to originate and direct human activities; in the other, it is the *action of person* for these ends.

Thus, one is said to be possessed of a *strong* Will (the *static)* when he is capable of exerting his mind with great force in a Volition or in a series of Volitions. The *quality* of his Will is manifest in the force and persistence of his Volitions or his acts. The manifested Will then becomes *dynamic*; his Volitions are the actions of the mind in self-direction.

Hence, the Will is to be regarded as an *energy,* and, according to its degree as such, it is weak, or fairly developed, or very great.

"It is related of Muley Moluc, the Moorish leader, that, when lying ill, almost worn out by incurable disease, a battle took place between his troops and the Portuguese, when, starting from his litter at the great crisis of the fight, he rallied his army, led them to victory, and then instantly sank exhausted, and expired."

Here was an exhibition of stored-up willpower.

So, also, Blondin, the rope-walker, said: "One day, I signed an agreement to wheel a barrow along a rope on a given day. A day or two before, I was seized by lumbago. I called in my medical man, and told him I must be cured by a certain day; not only because I should lose what I hoped to earn, but also forfeit a large sum. I got no better, and the evening before the day of the exploit, he argued against my thinking of carrying out my agreement. Next morning when I was no better, the doctor forbade me from getting up. I told him, 'What do I want with your advice? If you cannot cure me, of what good is your advice?' When I got to the place, the doctor was there, protesting that I was still unfit for the exploit. I went on, though I felt like a frog with my back. I got ready my the pole and barrow, took hold of the handles and wheeled it along the rope, as well as I ever did. When I got to the end of the rope, I wheeled it back again, and when this was done, I was a frog again. How did I wheel the barrow? *It was with my reserve-Will*".

Power of Will is, first, the mental capacity for a *single volitional act.* A powerful Will, as the saying goes, means the mind's ability to throw great energy into a given command for action, by itself, or by the body, or by other beings. This is what Emerson calls "the spasm to collect and swing the whole man".

The mind may, in this respect, be compared to an electric battery; discharges of force depending upon the size and make-up of the instrument; large amounts of force may be accumulated within it; and by proper manipulation an electric current of great strength may be obtained. There are minds that seem capable of huge exercise of willpower in single acts and under peculiar circumstances—as by the insane when enraged, or by ordinary people under the influence of excessive fear, or by exceptional individuals normally possessed of remarkable mental energy. So, power of Will may, as it were, be regarded as capable of accumulation. It may be looked upon as an energy that is susceptible of increase in quantity and of development in quality.

The Will is not only a dynamic force in mind, it is also secondly, a power of *persistent adherence to a purpose,* be that purpose temporary and not remote, or abiding and far afield in the future; whether it pertains to a small area of action or to a wide complexity of interests involving a life-long career. But what it is in persistence must depend upon what it is in any single *average* act of Volition. The Will may exhibit enormous energy in isolated instances while being utterly weak with reference to a continuous course of conduct or any great purpose in life. A mind that is weak in its average Volitions is incapable of sustained willing through a long series of actions or with reference to a remote purpose. The cultivation, therefore, of the Dynamic Will is essential to the possession of volitional power for a successful life.

"A chain is no stronger than its weakest link."

Development of Will has no other highway than absolute adherence to wise and intelligent resolutions.

The conduct of life hinges on the Will, but the Will depends upon the man. Ultimately, it is never other than his own election.

At this point appears the paradox of the Will: The Will is the soul's power of self-direction; yet the soul must decide how and for what purposes this power shall be exercised.

It is in such a paradox that questions of moral freedom have their origin. The freedom of the Will is a vexed problem, and can here receive only superficial discussion. The case seems to be clear enough, but it is too metaphysical for these pages.

Present Theory of Will

"The Will," says a French writer, "is to choose in order to act." This is not strictly true, for the Will does not choose at all. The person chooses. But in a general or loose way, the Will may be now defined as a power to choose what the man shall do. The choice is always followed by Volition, and Volition by appropriate action. To say that we choose to act in a certain way, while abstaining from so doing, is simply to say either that, at the instant of so abstaining, we do not choose, or that we cease to choose. We always do what we actually choose to do, so far as mental and physical abilities permit. When they do not permit, we may *desire,* but we do not *choose* in the sense of willing. In this sense, choice involves some *reason,* and such *reason* must always be *sufficient* in order to induce person to will.

A Sufficient Reason is a motive that the person approves as ground of action. This approval precedes the act of willing, that is, the Volition. The act of willing, therefore, involves choice among motives as its necessary precedent, and decision based upon such selection. When the mind approves a motive, that is, constitutes Sufficient Reason for its action in willing, it has thereby chosen the appropriate act obedient to willing. The mind frequently recognizes what, at first thought, might be regarded as Sufficient Reason for Volition, yet refrains from putting forth that Volition. In this case, other motives have instantaneously, perhaps unconsciously, constituted Sufficient Reason for inaction, or for action opposed to that immediately before considered.

We thus perceive four steps connected with the act of willing:

1. Presentation in mind of something that may be done;
2. Presentation in mind of motives or reasons relating to what may be done;
3. The rise in mind of Sufficient Reason;
4. Putting forth in mind of Volition corresponding to Sufficient Reason.

As Professor Josiah Royce remarks in "Outlines of Psychology", "We not only observe and feel our own doings and attitudes as a mass of inner facts, viewed all together, but in particular we attend to them with greater or less care, selecting now these, now those tendencies to action as the central objects in our experience of our own desires." "To attend to any action or to any tendency to action, to any desire, or to any passion, is the same thing as 'to select', or 'to choose', or 'to prefer', or 'to take serious interest in', just that tendency or deed. And such attentive (and *practical)* preference of one course of conduct, or of one tendency or desire, as against all others present to our minds at any time, is called a voluntary act." This is in effect the view of the author taken ten years before the writing of the first edition of the present work.

A motive is an appeal to person for a Volition. "A motive cannot be identified with the Volition to act, for it is the reason of the Volition. The identification of motives and Volitions would involve us in the absurdity of holding that we have as many

Volitions as motives, which would result in plain contradiction. "And, it may also be remarked," a motive is not an irresistible tendency, an irresistible tendency is not a desire, and a desire is not a Volition. In short, it is impossible to identify a Volition or act of Will with anything else. It is an act, *sui generis*[1]."

But while motives must be constituted Sufficient Reasons for willing, the reason is not a *cause*; it is merely an *occasion*. The *cause* of the act of Will is the person, free to select a reason for Volition. The *occasion* of the action of Volition in mind is solely the motive approved.

Motives are conditions; they are not causes. The testimony that they are not determining conditions stands on the validity of the moral consciousness. The word "ought" always preaches freedom, defying gospelers and metaphysicians of every pagan field.

Freedom

Moreover, the phrase "*freedom of will*" is tautology, and the phrase "*bondage of will*" is contradiction of terms. To speak of the freedom of the Will is simply to speak of the Will's existence. A person without power to decide what he shall do is not a complete organism.

Will may not exist, but if there is any Will in mind, it is free.

Will may be weak, but within the limitations of weakness, freedom nevertheless obtains.

No bondage exists in the power of person to will *somewhat*. Bondage may obtain in the man, by reason of physical disorders, or of mental incapacity, or of moral perversion, or, perhaps, of

---

[1]*Sui generis* is a Latin expression, literally meaning *of its own kind/genus* or unique in its characteristics. This expression is often used in analytic philosophy to indicate an idea, an entity, or a reality that cannot be included in a wider concept.

the environment. For the Will "does not sensate: that is done by the senses; it does not cognize: that is done by the intellect; it does not crave or loathe an object of choice: that is done by the affections; it does not judge of the nature, or value, or qualities of an object: that is done by the intellect; it does not moralize on the right or wrong of an object, or of an act of choice: that is done by the conscience (loosely speaking); it does not select the object to be chosen or to be refused, and set it out distinct and defined, known and discriminated from all others, and thus made ready, after passing under the review of all the other faculties, to be chosen or refused by the Will: for this act of selecting has already been done by the intellect."

The operations of the sense perceptions, of the intellect and of the moral powers may thus be inadequate, and there may be great difficulty in deliberating among motives, and even inability to decide which motive shall rule. But these weaknesses obtain in the mind or the man. They do not inhere in the Will. This does not surrender the freedom of the Will by shifting it from a faculty the definition of which makes it free to the person which may or may not be free, because any bondage of person has before it actual freedom as the result of development, education and moral influences. The action of Will is not determined by motive but by the condition of the person, and, to a degree, except under the oppression of disease, the person may always raise any motive to the dignity of Sufficient Reason.

Most people experience some bondage to evil, but the bondage of evil lies in the fact that the evil self tends to select a motive whose moral quality is of a like character. Accountability springs from this—that evil has been permitted to establish that tendency. "A force endowed with intelligence, capable of forming purposes and pursuing self-chosen ends may neglect those rules of action which alone can guide it safely, and thus at last wholly miss the natural ends of its being."

As Samuel Johnson says: "By trusting to impressions, a man

may gradually come to yield to them, and at length be subject to them, so as not to be a free agent, or, what is the same thing in effect, to *suppose* that he is not a free agent."

"As to the doctrine of necessity, no man believes it. If a man should give me arguments that I did not see, *though I could not answer them,* should I believe that I did not see?"

Hence the sway and the value of moral character in the arena of Will.

A person of right character tends to constitute right motives Sufficient Reason for Volitions.

The Will, therefore, is *under* law, for it is a part of the universal system of things. It must obey the general laws of man's being, must be true to the laws of its own nature. A lawless Will can have no assignable object of existence. As a function in mind, it is subject to the influences of the individual character, of environment and of ethical realities. But in itself, it discloses that all Volitions are connected with motives or reasons, that every Volition has its sufficient Reason, and that no Volition is determined solely by any given reason. To suppose the Will to act otherwise than as required by these laws is to destroy its meaning. A lawless Volition is not a free Volition, it is no Volition. Lawless Volition is caprice. Capricious Volitions indicate a mind subject to indeterminate influences. When an individual is in such a state, we say that he is a slave, because he is without power to act intelligently for a definite purpose and according to a self-chosen end.

Will is not free if it is not self-caused, but to be self-caused, in any true sense, it must act according to the laws of its own being. Law is the essence of freedom. Whatever is free is so because it is capable of acting out unhindered the laws of its nature.

The Will cannot transcend itself. It is not necessary that it should transcend its own nature in order to be free. A bird is free to fly, but not to pass its life under water. A bird with a broken wing cannot fly; nevertheless flight is of the freedom of bird-nature. And limitations upon bird-nature are not limitations upon such freedom. Induced limited states of individual minds cannot set aside the free ability of Will to act according to its fundamental nature.

The following, written of Howard the philanthropist, is a good illustration of the Will (*a*) as static, (*b*) as dynamic, *(c)* as an energy, (*d*) as controlled by the mind, *(e)* as free, and (*f*) as determined by character—what the individual makes himself to be:

"The *(c)* energy of his (*a*) determination was so great, that if, instead of being habitual, it had been (*b*) shown only for a short time on particular occasions, it would have appeared a vehement impetuosity; but, by being unintermitted, it had an equability of manner that scarcely appeared to exceed the tone of a calm constancy, it was so totally the reverse of anything like turbulence or agitation. It was the calmness of an intensity, *(d)* kept uniform by the nature of the human mind forbidding it to be more, and by the (*f*) character of the individual *(e)* forbidding it to be less."

Howard was an illustration of Emerson's meaning when he said: "There can be no driving force, except through the conversion of the man into his Will, making him the Will, and the Will him." Human nature is a huge commentary on this remark. Man's driving force, conquering fate, is the energy of the free Will.

Said Dr Edward H. Clarke: "The Will or Ego who is only known by his volitions, is a constitutional monarch, whose authority within certain limits is acknowledged throughout the system. If he chooses, like most monarchs, to extend his dominions and enlarge his power, he can do so. By a judicious exercise of his authority, employing direct rather than indirect measures, he can make every organ his cheerful subject. If, on the other hand, he is careless of his position, sluggish and weary of constant vigilance and labor, he will find his authority slipping from him, and himself the slave of his ganglia."

That you have a great world of opportunity awaiting your determination to possess it, is evidenced by this stirring view from the pen of C.G. Leland: "Now the man who can develop his will, has it in his power not only to control his moral nature to any extent, but also to call into action or realize very extraordinary states of mind, that is faculties, talents, or abilities which he never suspected to be within his reach. ...All that Man has ever attributed to the Invisible World without, lies, in fact, within him, and the magic key which will confer the faculty of sight and the power to conquer is the *Will.*"

We have now finished our brief survey of the theory of willpower. The idea has been to make clear to you the place which willpower occupies in your life—to stimulate you to an immediate, determined, and pleasurable, nay—profitable training in this kingly force within your possession.

What this book shall accomplish for the reader depends solely upon them.

CHAPTER II

TESTS OF WILL

The seat of the Will seems to vary with the organ through which it is manifested; to transport itself to different parts of the brain, as we may wish to recall a picture, a phrase, or a melody; to throw its force on the muscles or the intellectual processes. Like the general-in-chief, its place is everywhere in the field of action. It is the least like an instrument of any of our faculties; the farthest removed from our conceptions of mechanism and matter, as we commonly define them.

—O.W. Holmes

The developed Will manifests itself, as has been suggested, in two general ways.

First. In an energetic *single act*; here it may be called the *Dynamic Will.* The Will so acting is not necessarily ideal. "Rousseau," says Carlyle, "has not depth or width, nor calm force for difficulty—the first characteristic of true greatness. A fundamental error, to call vehemence and rigidity strength! A man is not strong who takes convulsion-fits, though six men cannot hold him then. He that can walk under the heaviest weight without staggering, he is the strong man."

Secondly. In a *series of acts* conducted with force and related intelligently to a given end; here the *Static Will discharges* in dynamic actions its store of accumulated power.

Acts of Will may be described as Explosive, Decisive, Impelling, Restraining, Deliberative, Persistent.

These forms of Will are exhibited in connection with Physical, Mental, Moral states of the man.

Remembering that the Will is always the mind's power of

self-direction, we now suggest certain:

General Functions of Will

I. The strong Will is master of the body.
II. The right Will is lord of the mind's several faculties.
III. The perfect Will is the high priest of the moral self.

I

The strong Will is master of the body, directing it according to the dictates of desire or reason. Hamlet's grave-digger determines his own physical vocation. The hero Dewey and his sailors send their bodies into Manila Bay and forbid flight, while shot and shell are falling. Martyrs give their bodies to be burned. Paganini directs his fingers to execute marvels upon the violin. The trained athlete is the director of an assembly of physical powers as difficult of original control as the mob that threatened Beecher at Liverpool. Ignatius uncovered brute Will when he said: "It is the part of a good athlete to be flayed with pounding, and yet to conquer." The psychic investigator of the modern college makes every physical element and power a tool, a prophet, a revelator of mental reality.

Mastery of the body is frequently seen in remarkable instances of *physical control.* All voluntarily acquired habits are examples. Though a given habit becomes automatic, it yet represents a long and persistent application of Will, and, as often, perhaps, the present exercise of Volition directing and maintaining actions that are apparently unconscious. The singer's use of his voice exhibits a trained impulse; the musician's manipulation of his fingers, habituated movements; the skilled rider's mastery of his limbs in the most difficult feats and unexpected situations, spontaneous response to the mind; the eloquent orator, celerity of muscular obedience to feeling. In all these and similar cases, the Will must act, coordinating particular movements with general details of Volition with the ultimate purpose in view. Indeed, the specific activities that make up the complex physical uses of the human body in all trades of skill demand supervision of the Will as an adequate explanation. The person may not be conscious of its sovereign acts, but it is the power upon the throne.

Underlying those states of the soul of which it is immediately aware are conditions not formulated in consciousness, which nevertheless constitute its highest powers. If these exhibitions of "second nature" involved no immediate action of Will, the very exercise and training of Will which look to their attainment would, so far forth, defeat the end in view; —they would weaken rather than develop Will.

The Unconscious or Subconscious Mind plays a vast role in human life. The reader is referred to the author's work "Practical Psychology" for further study of that important subject.

The mind, again, has the power to summon, as it were, a special degree of *intensity of Will*, and to throw this with great force into a particular act. This may be done during a repetition of the act, while the repetition is going on "automatically", as it is said. Does such intensity imply that no Will has hitherto been exerted? We know that in such cases we put forth a more energetic Volition.

The human eye may be made to blaze by the application of willpower to the act of gazing.

The hearing may be made more acute by willing that all other sensations shall be ruled out of consciousness.

By focusing the attention upon the terminal nerves, the sense of touch is vastly quickened, as, for example, in the case of the blind.

Muscular effort accomplishing a certain amount of work while Will is but lightly applied, becomes terrific when the whole man wills himself into the act.

Certain stimulations of the mind, such as fear, or love, or hate, or hope of reward, or religious excitement, or musical influence, or insanity, rouse the Will at times to vast proportions in its feats with muscle and limb.

The Olympic contests and modern exhibition games, rescues from fire or wave, woman's defense of her offspring, prolonged exertion of political speakers and evangelists, and Herculean achievements of enraged inmates of insane hospitals, furnish examples.

So, also, the Will accomplishes wonders through its *power of inhibition.* Under the fear of detection, the hiding criminal simulates the stillness of death. Pride often represses the cry of pain. In the presence of the desperately ill, love refuses the relief of tears. Irritated nerves are controlled under maddening conditions. Certain nervous diseases can be cured by the Will. Habits of the body, such as facial twitching, movements of the hands or limbs, etc., are controlled, and mannerisms of private and public life are banished. Sounds are shut out of consciousness in the act of reading. Strong appetites are denied indulgence. Pronounced tendencies in general physical conduct are varied. Attitudes of the body are assumed and maintained at the cost of great pain.

Even more than is ordinarily supposed, the body is the servant of the Will. The curious thing here is that so little attention is given to the training of Will in this capacity.

II

The right Will is the lord of the mind's several faculties. A familiar example is seen in the act of *attention.* Here, the soul concentrates its energies upon a single object, or upon a number of objects grouped together. A striking example may be noted in the fact that "we can smell either one of two odors, brought to the nostrils by means of paper tubes, in the preference to the other, by simply thinking about it." This is a good illustration of abstraction induced by the Will. The degree of exclusiveness and force with which the mind engages itself upon a single line of action represents the cultivation of the persistent Will. If the Will is strong in this respect, it is probably strong in what is called "*compound attention*", or that considering the state of mind in which it holds deliberative court among motives, facts, principles, means and methods relating to some possible end of effort or goal of conduct.

Thus, the person wills intense consciousness of physical acts or states. One, for example, who studies profoundly the relation of physiology to psychology, exhibits great powers in willed attention, embracing largest sensations, and taking note of minutest variations with the greatest nicety. The child in learning to walk manifests admirable ability in this regard. Vocal exercises demand utmost attention of the mind to musical notes, their effects upon the ear, and the manner and method of their attainment and execution. Musical instruments are also mastered in this way alone. All use of tools and instruments makes large demand upon the Will, and in proportion to their delicacy, complexity, and the difficulty of handling properly, is this demand increased. "Great skill, great Will," may be written as the general law in this regard.

So, also, as previously suggested, the power of the eye, ear and end nerves is frequently increased by application of mental energy thrown forcibly into the sense-perception involved.

The action and capacity of the lungs may be developed by intelligent attention, a style of walk may be cultivated, and habits of speech entirely reorganized. Where pronounced ability in such cases has been acquired, the cost of willed attention has been enormous.

A test of Will may be further seen in the degree of attention exerted in reading. In true reading, the mind is focused upon the printed page. Kossuth said, "I have a certain rule never to go on in reading anything without perfectly understanding what I read." That was true reading.

Equally concentrated must be the mind of the artist in painting, and that of the musician in mastering a difficult composition. An artist who painted three hundred portraits during a year, said: "When a sitter came, I looked at him attentively for half an hour, sketching from time to time on the canvas. I wanted no more. I put away my canvas and was ready for another sitter. When I wished to resume my first portrait, I took the man and sat him in the chair, when I saw him as distinctly as if he had been before me in his own proper person." A similar story is related of the sculptor David. Wishing to execute the bust of a dying woman without alarming her, he called upon her as a jeweler's man, and in a few moments, secured a mental portrait of her features, which he afterward reproduced in stone. So Blind Tom listened with "rapt attention" to a complicated musical composition, and instantly repeated it, exactly as played before him, including errors. In part, concentrated attention is the secret of genius.

In *sustained thinking*, the Will manifests one of its noblest aspects. The mind must now plunge into the depths of a subject, penetrate by driving force into its minutest details, and follow out the ramifications of its utmost complexities, concentrating upon fact, reality, relation, etc., with great power, and comparing, conjoining, separating, evolving, with tireless persistency. Napoleon was gigantic in all these particulars. Senator Carpenter, of Wisconsin, used to seclude himself in his law library the night before some important case was docketed for trial, and feel, think and care for nothing else until morning, utterly absorbed in the mastery of its problems. So Byron was wont to immure himself with brandy and water and write for many consecutive hours in the elaboration of his poems.

"The success of Hegel is in part explained by the fact that he took a manuscript to his publishers in Jena on the very day when the battle of that name was fought, and to his amazement—for he had heard or seen nothing—he found French veterans, the victorious soldiers of Napoleon, in the streets. Mohammed falling into lone trances on the mountains above Mecca, Paul in Arabia, Dante in the woods of Fonte Abellana, and Bunyan in prison, form eloquent illustrations of the necessity of mental seclusion and concentration in order to arrive at great mental results."

It is familiarly known that one of the secrets of concentration is *interest* in the matter in hand. But the mind's *interest may be enhanced* by persistent assertion of its power of Will. Study, resolutely continued, bores into the subject considered, and, discovering new features, finally induces absorbed attention of an increased degree. School-work furnishes many illustrations of this reward of Will. The mind may be wrought up, by long attention to matters of thought, to a state of great activity. As with mechanical contrivances, so with Will; initial movements of mind, weak at first, acquire by continuance an enhanced power." We can work ourselves up," as one has said, "into a loving mood, by forcing the attention and the train of ideas upon all the kindness and affection that we have experienced in the past." Similarly in regard to other emotions and states of the soul. The activity of reasoning is no exception. It is a mistake to suppose that great intellectual achievements are products alone of what is called "inspiration". The processes of reasoning, composing, speaking, all exhibit the power of Will to develop interest and beget a true inspiration as well as to hold the mind in the grip of a subject. Lord Macaulay thus sought facility in the preparation and writing of his History. Anthony Trollope made it a rule, while writing a work of fiction, to turn off a fixed number of pages each day, and found his rule not a hindrance, but a help. In jury trials, advocates talk on for hours against some supposedly obstinate juryman, and legislative halls frequently witness "speaking against time". In both cases, the orator's mind develops special and unexpected interest and power.

The strength of the Will is, again, notably shown in the action of *memory.* Mental energy usually "charges" the soul by the process of "memorizing". But some facts are blazed into the abiding self, as it were, by the power of great interest. The storing act of the mind in education, as it is commonly understood, requires Will in a very especial sense. Listless repetition of lessons accomplishes little. Attention, concentration, the forcing of interest, must take this kingdom by a kind of violence. A phrase like, "Remember! Yes, remember!" suggests the victorious attitude of the mind. Macaulay, fearing that his memory might fail, deliberately set himself to the task of its test and further development. William H. Prescott, who wrote his histories with greatly impaired eyesight, trained his memory so thoroughly that he could perform mentally the work required for sixty pages before dictation. Francis Parkman and Charles Darwin acquired prodigious memories under similar difficulties. Some minds are naturally endowed with great powers in this respect, but the really useful memories of the world exhibit the driving and sustaining action of Will.

Memory is always involved in *imagination.* The mind that is a blank as to its past can form no memory pictures. In its noblest character, the imagination exhibits compulsion, purpose, control. Milton must summon in luminous array the majestic images of "Paradise Lost". Does Angelo see his immortal shapes without the direction of Will? Do the phantoms of the ideal world come unbidden to the arena of thought? Undoubtedly, fantasies and hallucinations may troop across the plains of mental vision in capricious freedom, as when Luther saw the devil, or Goethe beheld in his sister's home a picture by Ostade; and these may frequently tyrannize over the mind with terrible power, as when Kipling's civilian of India became "possessed" by the "Phantom Rickshaw". But the hallucinations of disease often yield to treatment of physical improvement and resolute Will. It is significant that Goethe, relating the experience above referred to, says: "This was the first time that I discovered, in so high a degree, the gift, *which I afterwards used* with more complete consciousness, of bringing before me the characteristics of this or that great artist, to whose works I had devoted great attention." That the power of creating such luminous mental vision can be acquired by strenuous Will may be doubted; but there are minds that have frequent flashes of clear pictorial innersight, in which objects seem to appear with all the vividness of sunlit reality, although they can never command this experience at will. If possessed, the gift, as Goethe calls it, is, however, subject to summons and control, as seen in his case and in that of many artists. A secondary quality of mental vision, in which ideas of things, more or less vague and confused, and similar assemblages of objects, arise, is, by common testimony a matter of determined cultivation. Professions that require regular public speaking, as of the ministry or the law; the massing of facts before the mind, as in the trial of jury cases; the forming of material shapes and their organization into imaginary mechanisms, as in invention; the grasp of details and comprehensive plans, as in large business enterprises and military operations, all furnish illustrations of the truth that not original endowment alone, but energetic exercise of Will, is a requisite for success. Ideas, relations, objects and combinations may be made more vivid and real by resolution of the mind and persistent practise. Failures in these fields are frequently due to the fact that the Will does not force the mind to see things as details and as complex wholes. The strong Will enables the mind to recall, with growing intensity, objects, mechanisms, assemblages of facts and persons, outlines of territory, complex details and laws of enterprise, and airy fancies and huge conceptions of the worlds of real life and of ideal existence. The imagination is the pioneer of progress—in religion, industry, art and science; but as such it is not a lawless necromancer without deliberate purpose. The spirit that summons, guides and controls it is the soul's mysterious power of self-direction. And this power is equally susceptible of being so developed as to indicate selection and exclusion of clamoring images.

Hence, it would seem that *the mind may train and develop its own power of willing*. When cultivation and improvement of Will are sought, we may say, "*I will to will with energy and decision! I will to persist in willing! I will to will intelligently and for a goal! I will to exercise the Will according to the dictates of reason and of morals!*" Some men are born with what are called "strong Wills". If these are to be reasonable Wills as well, they must be trained. For the most part, Will would seem to develop and to acquire something of the "sweet quality of reasonableness", under life-processes that are more or less unconscious and unpurposed so far as this end is concerned; nevertheless, the exigencies of "getting on" are constant and unappreciated trainers. Discipline knocks men about with ruthless jocularity. "A man who fails, and will not see his faults, can never improve." Here is a grim-visaged, and oftentimes humorous schoolmaster who gives small pity to his pupils. They must acquire some power of Will or demonstrate themselves, not human, but blockheads. Much of life's suffering is due to the fact that force of Will is neither developed nor trained by conscious intelligent effort, and is more often devoid than possessed of rational moral quality. This is a curious thing—that the Will is left, like Topsy, "to grow up". Why value this power, yet take it "catch-as-catch-can"? Why hinge success upon it, yet give it so little conscious attention? Why delegate its improvement to the indirection of "hard knocks", and disappointment cankering resolution, and misfortune making water of life's blooded forces, and all manner of diseases destroying the fine fiber of mind's divine organism? Why neglect the Will until consequence, another name for hell, oftentimes, has removed "heaven" by the diameter of the universe?

James Tyson, a Bushman in Australia, died with a fortune worth $25,000,000. "But," he said, with a characteristic semi-exultant snap of the fingers, "the money is nothing. It was the little game that was the fun!" Being asked once, "What was 'the little game'?" he replied with an energy of concentration peculiar to him: "Fighting the desert. That has been my work. I have been fighting the desert all my life, and I have won! I have put water where was no water, and beef where was no beef. I have put fences where there were no fences, and roads where there were no roads. Nothing can undo what I have done, and millions will be happier for it after I am long dead and forgotten."

"The longer I live," said Fowell Buxton, whose name is connected in philanthropy with that of Wilberforce, "the more certain I am that the great difference between men, between the feeble and the powerful, the great and the insignificant, is Energy—Invincible Determination—a purpose once fixed, and then Death or Victory. That quality will do anything that can be done in this world—and no talents, no circumstances, no opportunities will make a two-legged creature a Man without it." The power, then, of such resistless energy should with resistless energy be cultivated.

"When the Will fails, the battle is lost."

III

The perfect Will is the high Priest of the moral self. Indeed, a true cultivation of Will is not possible without reference to the highest reason or ideas of right. In the moral consciousness alone is discovered the explanation of this faculty of the soul. A great Will may obtain while moral considerations are ignored, but no perfection of Will can be attained regardless of requirements of the highest reason. The crowning phase of the Will is always ethical.

CHAPTER III

THE CONDUCT OF LIFE

Resolve is what makes a man manifest; not puny resolve, not crude determinations, not errant purpose—but that strong and indefatigable Will which treads down difficulties and danger, as a boy treads down the heaving frost-lands of winter; which kindles his eye and brain with a proud pulse-beat toward the unattainable. Will makes men giants.

—Ik Marvel

The thing that is, and creates human power, as the author remarks in "Business Power", is the Will. Theoretically, the Will is the man. Practically, the Will is just a way the man has of being and doing. The Will is man's inherent nature-tendency to act—to do something. This tendency to act in some way must act on itself—take itself in hand, so to speak, in order that it may act intelligently, continuously, and with a purpose. Will is itself power; but unfolded, controlled and directed power in man is Will self-mastered, not man-mastered nor nature-mastered. The man-mastered and nature-mastered Will goes with the motive or impulse that is the strongest. The self-mastered Will goes with the motive that the self makes greatest, and with mere impulse in very slight degree so far as the life of intelligence is concerned.

The self-mastered Will can do anything—within reason; and reason in this connection should be conceived in its highest human sense. The function of Will is like that of steam. It must be powerful, under control, and properly directed. The power of Will may be developed, but only through controlled and directed action. The control may be acquired, but only through willed and directed action. The direction may be determined, but only through willed and controlled action. When Will is self-developed, self-mastered, self-directed, it only needs proper application to become practically all-powerful.

Forms of Will

In the conduct of life, every form in which the normal Will manifests itself is demanded for success. These forms are: (i) The Persistent Will; (ii) The Static Will; (iii) The Impelling Will; (iv) The Dynamic Will; (v) The Restraining Will; (vi) The Explosive Will; (vii) The Decisive Will.

The *Static Will,* or Will in reserve, constitutes original source of energy. As heat, light, and life are rooted in the sun, so are varied Volitions sent forth from this central seat of power, exhibiting the *Dynamic Will.*

The *Explosive Will* illustrates the mind's ability for quick and masterful summoning of all its forces. The sudden rush of the whole soul in one compelling deed seems sometimes next to omnipotence.

Persistence of Will involves "standing", *sto—stare—sistere,* and "through"—*per*; "standing through." The weakness of otherwise strong men may be revealed in life's reactions. "Having done all, to stand," furnishes many a deciding test. This phase of Will is not exhausted in the common saying, "sticking to it", for a barnacle sticks, and is carried hither and thither on a ship's bottom. Persistence involves adherence to a purpose clean through to a goal.

The *abiding mind* necessitates the *Impelling Will.* The Impelling Will suggests an ocean "liner", driving onward, right onward, through calm and storm, for a determined goal. Sixty years of that kind of direct motion must summon Will to all its varied activities.

It is curious, too, that the noble quality of Willpower observed in impelling persistence, depends upon the paradox of restraint. An engine without control will wreck itself and its connected machinery. The finest racing speed is achieved under bit and mastery. In man, the power that drives must hold back. The supremest type of man exhibits this as a constant attitude. Success in life depends upon what the writers call the Will's power of inhibition. Here, we have the *Restraining Will.*

At times, the character of Will is also manifested in its ability to forbid obedience to a thousand appealing motives, and even to bring all action to a full stop and "back water", in a new decision, a new immediate or ultimate goal. Hence life is full of demands for quick decisions and resistless massing of resources squarely upon the spur of exigency. This suggests the *Decisive Will.*

Such are some of the forms of Will required for the conduct of affairs, whether ordinary or extraordinary. Even a slight analysis of the matter would seem to suggest that there can be no tonic like the mental mood that resolves to will.

Here is a treatment from the deepest laboratories of the soul insuring health. A purposeful mind says, sooner or later, "I Resolve To Will". *After a time, that phrase is in the air, blows with the wind, shines in stars and the sun, sings with rivers and seas, whispers with dreams of sleep and trumpets through the hurly-burly of day. Eventually, it becomes a feeling of achievement saturating consciousness. The man knows now the end, because all prophecies have one reading. He has begotten the instinct of victory.*

It is not as a blind man, however, that he walks. His ineradicable conviction sees with the eye of purpose. If his purpose is approvable at the court of conscience, all roads lead to his Rome.

One Aim Victorious

Men fail for lack of *Some Aim.* Their desires cover the entire little field of life, and what becomes theirs does so by accident. Multitudes of people are the beneficiaries of blundering luck.

Everywhere *Some Aim* would make "hands" foremen, and foremen superintendents; would conduct poverty to comfort, and comfort to wealth; would render men who are of no value to society useful, and useful men indispensable.

The man who is indispensable owns the situation.

The world is ruled by its servants. The successful servant is king.

But better than *Some Aim,* which, because it need be neither long-headed nor long-lived, is a player at a gaming table, *One Aim,* by which all fortune is turned schoolmaster and good fortune is labeled "reward by divine right". The true divine right of kings is here alone.

The soul that resolves to will *One Aim* makes heavy and imperious call on the nature of things.

For, while many understand that the individual must adjust himself to life, few perceive the greater law, that *life is forever engaged in a desperate struggle to adjust itself to the individual.* It is but required of him that he treats life with some degree of dignity, and makes his election and plea sure by putting mind in the masterful spell of some *One* ultimate *Aim* to which all things else shall be subordinated.

Some Aim has luck on its side; *One Aim* has law.

Some Aim may achieve large things, and occasionally it does; *One Aim* cannot fail to make the nature of things its prime minister.

Life does not always yield the *One Aim* its boon in exact terms of desire, because men often fall at cross-purposes with endowment; but life never fails to grant all the equities in any given case.

In the long run, every man gets in life what he deserves. The vision of that truth embraces many things that the objector will not see. The objector mistakes what he desires for what he deserves.

Hence the importance of self-discovery in life's conduct. It is probably true that every man has some one supreme possibility within his make-up. The purposeful Will usually discovers what it is.

Buried talents are always "fool's gold".

One thing settled—the *Ultimate Aim*—and talents begin to emerge by a divine fiat.

The revelation of power may, indeed, be made while Will roams in quest of a purpose, but, that purpose found, Will looks for its means and methods; and discovers them within.

William Pitt was, in fact, born with a definite aim in life. "From a child," says a recent writer, "he was made to realize that a great career was expected of him, worthy of his renowned father. This was the keynote of all his instruction."

General Grant is said to have been called "Useless Grant" by his mother. He discovered himself at Shiloh, after some pottering with hides and leather which was not even preliminary. But Grant always "stuck to the thing in hand," so far as it was worth while doing so. When war brought his awareness of self to the point of definite meaning, he found every detail and the largest campaigns eminently worth the while of a Will which had at last uncovered its highway. "The great thing about him," said Lincoln, "is cool persistency of purpose. He is not easily excited, and he has got the grip of a bulldog. When he gets his teeth in, nothing can shake him off."

The *One Aim* is always a commentary on character. It is not difficult to see why life needs *Some Aim*. Why it should concentrate upon *One Aim* suggests the whole philosophy of human existence. Nero had *One Aim*, and it destroyed the half of Rome. Alexander the Great had *One Aim*, and he died in a debauch. The *One Aim* may involve selfishness, crimes, massacres, anarchy, universal war, civilization hurled to chaos. *One Aim* assassinated Garfield, ruined Spain, inaugurated the Massacre of Saint Bartholomew, gave birth to the "unspeakable Turk", devised a system of enmity against existing orders and institutions, threatened to throw Europe into revolutionary carnage, and, in a thousand ways, had power to light the pyre of civilization's destruction. *One Aim* is no more descriptive of Heaven than it is of Hell.

The climax of Will, therefore, is possible under moral considerations alone. Character, which is the sum total of a man's good (moral) qualities, furnishes a third phrasing for Will's purpose, the *Righteous Aim.*

The Highest Aim

Will with *Righteous Aim* creates character. Character, with *Righteous Will,* creates *Noblest Aim.* Character, with *Noblest Aim,* creates *Righteous Will.*

The relation between the man, the aim, the Will, is dependent and productive. There is really no high justification for *One Aim* if it be not best aim. Life is ethical. Its motives and its means and its achievements justify only in aims converging to its utmost moral quality.

It is here that possession of Will finds explanation, as elsewhere remarked. Below man, there is no supreme sovereignty of Will; all is relative and reflex. But this sovereignty furnishes its reason in moral self-development, in moral community-relations, in moral oneness with Deity.

So true is it that *righteousness alone justifies the existence of the human Will,* that the finest development of the power comes of its moral exercise. Above the martyr who founds a material government the world places with eager zeal that soul who establishes by his death a kingdom of religion.

The Static Will furnishes energy in abnormal life. The Explosive Will murders. The Persistent Will may exhibit in obstinacy and national crimes. The Impelling Will is sometimes hugely reckless. The Restraining Will has its phases in "mulishness" and stupidity. The Decisive Will is frequently guilty of wondrous foolhardiness.

Idiocy, insanity, senility, savagery and various forms of induced mania represent the Will in disorder, without a master, and working pathos fathomless or tragic horror.

If, then, we ask, "Why *One Aim* in life?" the names of Socrates, Buddha, Charlemagne, Alfred the Great, William of Orange, Gladstone, Washington, Wilberforce and Lincoln, may be offset by those of Caligula, the Medici, Lucrezia Borgia and Philip the Second. Asking, "Why the *Righteous Aim*?" troop before the mind's expanding eye all holy heroes and movements "I' the tide o' time"; and no counterpoise appears, for all is great, all is good.

Moral purpose, however, is no prestidigitator. The Will, set on all good things for ultimate goal, is still merely the mind's power of self-direction. All requisites for strong Will anywhere are demands here. Inasmuch as the moral aim involves the whole of life, Will, making for it, requires the ministry of cultivated perceptions: seeing things as they are, especially right things; developed sensibilities: sensitive toward evil, capacious for good; a large imagination: embracing details, qualities, consequences, reasons and ultimate manifold objects; active, trained and just reasoning faculties: apprehending the incentive, utility and inspiration of truth; and deep and rich moral consciousness : nourishing the Will from inexhaustible fountains of legitimate self-complacency.

In other words, the moral Will, which alone is best Will, demands of its owner constant and adequate consideration, of plan, of means, of methods, of immediate and ultimate end.

The successful conduct of life is always hinged upon "This one thing I do." Where such is really the law of conduct, the world beholds an aroused soul. "The first essential of success," said a great bank president, "is the fear of God."

A live man is like a factory working on full time. Here is creation; every power at labor, every function charged with energy, huge action dominating the entire situation, and yielding valuable products. This man puts his body into the thing in hand, mightily confident. His mental being does not detail itself off in "gangs", but swarms at it with that tirelessness which makes enthusiasm a wonder. His intuitions flash, impel, restrain, urge resistlessly, decide instantly—presiding genii of limited empires. Reasoning faculties mass upon questions vital, and hold clear court, till justice be known. If he be a right-souled man, he emerges, Will at the fore, from Decalogue and Mountain Sermon daily, squaring enterprise with the Infinite.

The *whole man,* swinging a great Will, *conserves himself.*

Why must there be discussions on selfishness and self-interest? A sound soul is always the best soul. A selfish soul is never sound. But a sound soul must continue sound. Altruism begins with the self. Society needs the whole man—all there is of him, and always at his best. Hence, the nature of things makes it law that a man shall endeavor to make the most of himself in every way which is not inimical to soundness. This is the first principle of holiness—wholeness—soundness. As that is worked into conduct, the second principle appears—Service.

For the service of a sound soul the Universe will pay any price.

And here again emerge some old and common rules. It is function of Will to resolve on preservation of bodily health, mental integrity and growth, and moral development. In the eye of that high resolution, no detail is without importance. A trained Will regards every detail as a campaign.

Drudgery and the Will

Power of Will is an accretion. Force is atoms actively aggregated. The strong Will is omnivorous, feeding upon all things with little discrimination. Pebbles, no less than boulders, compose mountains. The man who cannot will to stick to trifles and bundle them into importants, is now defeated. The keynote of success is drudgery.

Drudgery stands at every factory door, and looks out of every store window. If drudgery be not somewhere in a book, it is not worth the reading. Inspiration stands tip-toe on the back of poor drudgery. The antecedents of facile and swift art are the aches and sorrows of drudgery. The resistance of angels collapses only after Jacob has found his thigh out of joint, and yet cries: "I will not let thee go!" Jesus had to climb even Calvary.

An English Bishop said truly: "Of all work that produces results, nine-tenths must be drudgery." Really great poets, prose-writers and artists verify this remark. Edmund Burke bestowed upon his speeches and addresses an immense amount of painstaking toil. Macaulay's "History" cost almost incalculable labor. The first Emperor of Germany was an enormous worker. Indeed, taking the world "by and large", labor without genius is little more incapable than genius without labor.

Kepler, the astronomer, carried on his investigations with prodigious labor. In calculating an opposition of Mars, he filled ten folio pages with figures, and repeated the work ten times, so that seven oppositions required a folio volume of 700 pages. It has been said that "the discoveries of Kepler were secrets extorted from nature by the most profound and laborious research."

It was the steadiness of Haydn's application to his art which made him one of the first of modern musicians. He did not compose haphazardly, but proceeded to his work regularly at a fixed hour every day. These methods, with the extremest nicety of care in labor, gave him a place by the side of Mozart, who, while possessed of the genius of facility, was nevertheless thoroughly acquainted with drudgery.

And there can be no drudgery without patience, the ability to wait, constancy in exertion with an eye on the goal. Here is a complex word which readily splits into fortitude, endurance and expectation. It is kaleidoscopic in its variations. In the saint's character, patience is a lamb; in that which builds an industry or founds an empire, it is a determined bulldog.

"Genius is patience," said Davy; "what I am I have made myself." Grant was patient: "Once his teeth got in, they never let go." The assiduous Will is the first principle in achievement, whether of men or of nations. The indefatigable purpose is the prophet of all futures.

But the "King on his Throne" (your Will) is no dull monarch of obstinacy. Reason defies inertia. "We say that Will is strong whose aim," remarks Th. Ribot, "whatever it be, is fixed. If circumstances change, means are changed; adaptations are successfully made, in view of new environments; but the center toward which all converges does not change. Its stability expresses the permanency of character in the individual."

All things come to the net of this rational indefatigability. As Carlyle says of Cromwell: "That such a man, with the eye to see, with the heart to dare, should advance, from post to post, from victory to victory, till the Huntington Farmer became, by whatever name you might call him, the acknowledged strongest man in England, requires no magic to explain it. For this kind of man, on a shoemaker's bench or in the President's chair, is always 'Rex, Regulator, Roi'; or still better, 'King, Koenig', which means Can-ning, Ableman."

And this same adaptive pursuit of the main thing has made of Cromwell's and Carlyle's England the First Power in Europe. As William Mathews has said: "The 'asthmatic skeleton' (William III) who disputed, sword in hand, the bloody field of Landon, succeeded at last, without winning a single great victory, in destroying the prestige of his antagonist (Louis XIV), exhausting his resources, and sowing the seeds of his final ruin, simply by the superiority of British patience and perseverance. So, too, in the war of giants waged with Napoleon, when all the great military powers of the continent went down before the iron flail of the 'child of destiny', like ninepins, England wearied him out by her pertinacity, rather than by the brilliancy of her operations, triumphing by sheer dogged determination over the greatest master of combination the world ever saw."

It was identically this that led, in American history, to the surrender of Cornwallis to Washington, and to the last interview with Lee, a great soul, an heroic Christian fighter, a consummate "Can-ning man, Able-man".

To a Will of this sort defeats are merely new lights on reason, and difficulties are fresh gymnastics for development of colossal resolve, and discouragements are the goading stimuli of titanic bursts of energy.

"By means of a cord, which passes from his artificial hand up his right coat-sleeve, then across his back, then down his left coat-sleeve to the remainder of his left arm, an American editor has achieved success. He is enabled to close the fingers of his artificial hand and grasp his pen. By keeping his left elbow bent, the tension of the string is continued, and the artificial fingers hold the pen tightly, while the editor controls its course over the paper by a movement of the upper arm and shoulder. By this means, without arms, he has learned to write with the greatest ease, and more rapidly and legibly than the average man of his age who has two good hands. For ten years, he has written with this mechanical hand practically all of the editorials, and a very large amount of the local and advertising matter that has gone into his paper."

"Suppose," said Lord Clarendon to Cyrus W. Field, talking about the proposed Atlantic Cable, "you don't succeed? Suppose you make the attempt and fail—your cable is lost in the sea—then what will you do?" "Charge it to profit and loss, and go to work to lay another."

To suppose the iron Will to fail is to suppose a contradiction of terms.

Perhaps no historic character has more perfectly illustrated this element of success than William of Orange, to whom Holland the Wonderful owes more than to any other son in her brilliant family. "Of the soldier's great virtues," writes Motley, "constancy in disaster, devotion to duty, hopefulness in defeat—no man ever possessed a larger share. That with no lieu tenant of eminent valor or experience, save only his brother Louis, and with none at all after that chieftain's death, William of Orange should succeed in baffling the efforts of Alva, Requesens, Don John of Austria, and Alexander Farnese—men whose names are among the most brilliant in the military annals of the world—is in itself sufficient evidence of his warlike ability."

These men, great and world-famed, were, however, men only. They were but Intellects working with the "King on his Throne". It is a statement which points every other man to his ultimate goal that they achieved through that common endowment, power of Will.

The conduct of life hinges on the strength and quality of Will more than any other factor. The cry for "opportunity" is essentially weak; opportunity crowds upon the imperious Will. The mediocrity of men is too largely of their own creation.

Gladstone, with large faith in the "commoners", said truly:

"In some sense and in some effectual degree, there is in every man the material of good work in the world; in every man, not only in those who are brilliant, not only in those who are quick, but in those who are stolid, and even in those who are dull."

Every normal educated man, deep in his heart believes that by the proper conduct of his life, he can become great—or at least win a measure of success that puts him far ahead of the mediocre millions. But as "rest and inertia" is the law of matter, he gradually gives in to this law and is shackled by it. He becomes, speaking "in the large", too lazy to forge on toward the higher goals. It is here that incessant use of willpower is required.

"The education of the will should be begun, contradictory as it may seem, by assuring yourself you can do what you wish to do, and assuring yourself on the principles of auto-suggestion. Of course, no amount of willpower can accomplish impossible aims.... By 'what you wish to do', we mean the ambitions proper to your intelligence and place in life. Not to set yourself an impossible task, is half the battle. A mighty will with no intelligence behind it is foiled everywhere; and without scruple it becomes a menace to the world's peace. So 'choose right', and move forward."

CHAPTER IV

DISEASES OF THE WILL

'Mechanical obedience' (in the treatment of disease—and of mind as well as of body) is but one-half the battle; the patient must not only will, he must believe. The whole nature of man must be brought to the task, moral as well as physical, for the seat of the disease is not confined to the body; the vital energies are wasted; the Will, often the mind, are impaired. Fidelity of the body is as nothing if not reinforced by fidelity of the soul.

—Dr Salisbury

The Will may become diseased. Disease is "want of ease", that is, of comfort, arising from the failure of functions to act in a normal manner. It is, then, "any disorder or depraved condition or element," physical, mental or moral.

A disease of the Will may be defined as a more or less permanent lack of action, normal, (*a*) to the individual, (*b*) to sound human nature in general. When a person's Will is more or less permanently disordered with reference to his normal individual activity, we have a case for medical treatment. When a person's Will is more or less permanently disordered with reference to the normal human standard, we have a case for education.

It is now to be observed that a diseased condition of the Will may result—

First, from a diseased mind;

Secondly, from an illy developed mind;

Thirdly, from causes resident in the Will considered as a "faculty" of mind. Strictly speaking, a disease of the Will is a disease of the self, inasmuch as it is the self that wills. But there are phases of the Will, practically to be regarded as diseases, which manifest themselves in the midst of otherwise normal conditions of mind, and these are, therefore, mentioned under the third division above.

Classes of Diseased Will

I

Class First: Diseases of Will coming under the head of diseased mind are shown in *insanity.* In almost all cases of mental variation from the normal standard, the Will is more or less affected. This follows because insanity is "a *prolonged* departure of the individual's normal standard of thinking, feeling and acting". The standard is that of the *individual,* not that of normal human nature. Always the action of the Will depends largely upon the individual's way of thinking and feeling. Insanity often clearly defines, and thus separates from, diseases of Will in the so-called normal mind. In cases of insanity, the Will, considered as power in mind to put forth some kind of Volition, may remain with more or less strength, but is either weakened or controlled by physiological conditions or false ideas. The "King" is here dethroned. In diseases of Will which are subject to education not medical, the "King" remains in his normal position as ruler, but is weak, or erratic, or permanently irrational as to the standard of average human conduct.

II

Class Second: There are some cases of diseased Will in the *illy developed mind* which show paralysis of power, all other functions remaining normal. Thus, a sudden great emotion may paralyze the volitional action, such as fear, or anger, or joy. Inability to will may also obtain temporarily in reverie or ecstasy, or as seen in curious experiences common to most people when the self wishes to act, but seems for the time unable to put forth the necessary Volition. Such paralysis runs all the way from momentary to prolonged or total. In the latter cases, we have again subjects for medical treatment, as when one person was two hours into trying to get his coat off, or was unable to take a glass of water that was offered.

Whether the difficulty in cases of illy developed mind is physiological, or a mere lack of belief in one's power to will a given act, the outcome is the same. For the time being, the Will is dead, or the mind, as to willing, is in a state of deadlock. It cannot put forth a Volition in the desired direction. Hence, it is evident that feeling, desire, thinking, judgment and conscience are not always determinative of Will-action. The action of the mind in willing is as distinct as the action of the mind in imagining, recalling, reasoning, or apprehending right and wrong. For example, why, in a state of indecision as to getting up on a cold winter morning, do you suddenly find yourself shivering on the floor and wondering how it happened that you are out of bed? It needs but to fix that state of irresolution or inability for a period, to show the mind in a deadlock of the Will.

Willing is a matter of mental states. The illy developed self may will neither correctly nor strongly. Whether or not it can do so depends upon many things which are discussed in the Third Part of this book. Of the mind in general, it is said that "willing, in intensity ranges up and down a scale in which are three degrees—wishing, purposing and determining. Weak Volition wishes, resolute Volition purposes, while strong Volition acts." But Volition does not wish; this is an act of the mind. As one has said: "I may desire meat, or drink, or ease from pain ; but, to say that I will meat, or will drink, or will ease from pain, is not English." Weak Volition is the Will exerting itself weakly. Strong Volition indicates mental energy in the act of willing. Resolute Volition is strong Volition continued. The facts in this connection are as follows:

When the state of mind is predominantly that of desire merely, its act in willing may be weak or indecisive. When the mind greatly approves a given desire and determines that to be purpose, its Volition becomes strong. The energy with which itself or the body obeys Volition, and if the purpose is remote, continues to obey, measures the intensity of the willing act.

Now, what are called diseases of the Will under our second division, are simply ill conditions of the self immediately going out in the act of willing, or of the mind engaged in the realm of the sensibilities, the imagination, the reasoning faculties and the moral consciousness as realities capable of influencing the action of the Will.

For "the ultimate reason of choice is partly in the character, that is to say, in that which constitutes the distinctive mark of the individual in the psychological sense, and differentiates him from all other individuals in the same species," and partly in possible ideals, following which he may more or less change that distinctive character.

"It is the general tone of the individual's feelings, the general tone of his organism, that is the first and true motor. If this is lacking, the individual cannot exercise Will at all. It is precisely because this fundamental state is, according to the individual constitution, stable or fluctuating, continuous or variable, strong or weak, that we have three principal types of Will—strong, weak and intermittent, with all intermediate degrees and shades of differences between the three. But these differences, we repeat, spring from the character of the individual, and that depends upon his special constitution." And it is precisely because "this fundamental state is, according to the individual constitution," subject to education and improvement, so that, if fluctuating, it may become stable, if variable it may become continuous, if weak, it may become strong, that this book is written.

A good Will may or may not act quickly: that depends upon

the individual's constitution; but it is marked by power when it does act.

A good Will may or may not persist: that depends upon the constitution and the dictates of personal wisdom; but when personal wisdom succeeds in influence, the Will holds steadfastly to the thing in hand.

The highest type of Will reveals "a mighty, irrepressible passion which controls all the thoughts of the man. This passion *is* the man—the psychic expression of his constitution as nature made it." Historic examples are seen in Caesar, Michelangelo and Napoleon.

In the next lower grade, the above harmony between the outer conduct and the inner purpose is broken by various groups of tendencies, working together, but opposing the central purpose. The man is switched off the main track. Francis Bacon was called "the greatest, the wisest and the meanest of mankind", having diverged from the highest line of rectitude, and Leonardo da Vinci, following Art, yet yielded to the seductions of his inventive genius, and produced but one masterpiece.

A third grade is seen where two or more main purposes alternately sway the individual, none ruling for long, each influencing the conduct in turn. Dr Jekyll and Mr Hyde are two beings in one person, each possessing a strong Will for himself, but unable to cope with the tendencies of the other. A multiplication of such diverting purposes denotes a still further degradation of the Will.

Lastly appear those types of diseased Will peculiar to insanity.

III

Class Third: In this division, we have before us, not the mind as acting, but the willing act of the mind. Whether the Will be exercised rightly or wrongly, wisely or foolishly, is not now the question in hand. That question refers simply to Willpower, or the naked Will; just as, if an individual's muscular power were in question, the morality or the wisdom of its use might be variously estimated, itself being swift or slow, weak or strong, capable of endurance or easily exhausted. The Will is what it is, regardless of the direction or the quality of its exercise.

Disease of Will, as considered in the *third class,* is limited to two general forms: *want of power* and *want of stability.*

But these general divisions resolve themselves into more *specific cases,* as follows.

1. *Want of Volitional Impulse.* A state of mind in which the impulse to will is wanting is illustrated in the cases already cited, in which one could not get his coat off; or in cases of reverie, ecstasy, etc., where the mind is so fully absorbed by some fanciful condition as to be momentarily incapable of willing contrary thereto.

Cure: Of insane cases, medical treatment; of those of reverie, ecstasy, and the like, good health, full life and vigorous action. For the mind that suffers the deadlock of Will there is no other remedy than actual, concrete life, and practical, strenuous activity.

Cultivate the Moods of Resolution and Decision. (See Chapter VI.)

2. *Inability to Decide.* Some people never attain to a clear view of any situation; they cannot see the essential details; they cannot weigh motives; they cannot forecast the future; they are wanting in courage as to possible consequences; their imagination is good for evils, but not for benefits; hence they can never, or rarely, come to a definite, decisive determination. They drift; they do not act according to specific determinations; they are creatures of momentary impulse; they are *automata,* so far as concerns the ordinary affairs of life, and, in its extraordinary crises, they are as helpless as driftwood.

Cure: Cultivate the habit of concentrated attention to the thing in hand, pro and con; resolve to will, anyhow, somehow, with the best light rapidly examined, confident that such resolution, under the lessons of experience, will ultimately come out best for individual interests.

"Sometimes, a person encounters emergencies where he must make a decision, although aware that it is not a mature decision, approved by the whole cabinet of his mental powers. In that case, he must bring all his comprehension and comparison into active, instant exercise, and feel that he is making the best decision he can at the time, and act. Many important decisions of life are of this kind—off-hand decisions."

And especially ought it to be remembered that "calling upon others for help in forming a decision is worse than useless. A man must so train his habit as to rely upon his own courage in moments of emergency."

Act always on the straight line.

Cultivate the Mood of Decision.

3. *Weakness of Volition.* The failures of life, which are innumerable, are largely due to this disorder of the Will. Whether it be owing to a want of feeling, desire, imagination, memory or reason, it seems to be universal. The energetic person is the exception. Thus, a writer on Mental Philosophy has described a historic example of this prevalent disease; speaking of Coleridge: "There was probably never a man endowed with such remarkable gifts who accomplished so little that was worthy of them—the great defect of his character being the want of Will to turn his gifts to account; so that, with numerous gigantic projects constantly floating in the mind, he never brought himself even seriously to attempt to execute any one of them. It used to be said of him, that whenever either natural obligation or voluntary undertaking made it his duty to do anything, the fact seemed a sufficient reason for his *not* doing it."

So De Quincey, the celebrated victim of the opium habit, said in his "Confessions":

"I seldom could prevail upon myself to write a letter; an answer of a few words, to any that I received, was the utmost that I could accomplish; and often that not until the letter had lain weeks, or even months on my writing-table."

Such are historic examples of Willpower so weak as to be practically nil. They are common in life, although seldom in so marked a degree as in the above cases. This disease is the basis of all grades of poverty.

Cure: Cultivate the sustained mental attitude—"I Resolve to Will!" The Resolute Mood ought to be kept constantly before and in the mind, with *inability to will* as the *paramount reason* for *determining now to will* with the greatest energy.

Cultivate the Mood of Energy.

4. *Fickleness of Will.* In this case, the man is persistent so far as he goes, but he never goes far in any one direction. In certain main or underlying lines of activity, he may show great apparent steadfastness, as in pursuing the means of a livelihood, but these lines are necessitated and automatic or habitual, not really the subjects of his Volitions. There are those, too, who exhibit not even the dumb adherence of labor, but fly from scheme to scheme, whether main or incidental, as birds fly from tree to tree, with no long-continued purpose, during the whole course of life. In this class, the Will is subject to every new impulse.

Cure: The cautious beginning; the resolute pursuit of the undertaking to the end. Minds thus afflicted should learn to attend to one thing at a time, not in the sense that only a single iron should be kept in the fire, but that the iron should not be put there without due deliberation, and that once in, it should receive undivided attention so long as required by the end in view. Generally speaking, every supposed reason for a change of action should be made a determining reason for not changing. The extra schemes need not be given up; it is not necessary for any person to settle down to the mere drudgery of existence; but, while following the course of bread-winning, the mind should determine, *resolve*, Swear, to work each theory or scheme to the end thereof.

Cultivate the Mood of Continuity.

5. *Want of Perseverance.* There is a marked difference between this condition of Will and that of fickleness. Will is fickle because it yields to sudden or new impulses. Want of perseverance is due to the fact that the *Will wears out* in any given direction. It then becomes like a tired muscle; the mind refuses or fails to volitionate with reference to an old purpose. Its characteristic phrase is, "I am tired of the thing," or "I can't hold out in the effort." Resolution has simply run down; the Will has become exhausted.

Cure: The resolution to refrain from yielding permanently to such momentary exhaustion; patience with the mind's present inertia; vigorous search, carried on round-about, for new points of view and new interest. The saying, "I am tired of it," indicates simply a temporary lack of interest; willed interest has failed; but a new view or another mental attitude may inspire spontaneous interest; hence, the matter should be held over until the search for new interest has awakened a spontaneous action of the Will, which will almost invariably follow. This cure is infallible; but it is by no means easy.

Cultivate the Moods of Understanding, Reason and Continuity.

6. *The Explosive Will.* Any explosion indicates want of equilibrium. Great temper, unpremeditated crime and volcanic Volitions are sudden releases of energy revealing an overcharged or unbalanced nervous tone. With some men power is always in what may be called a chemico-psychical state of instability. The Will leaps to its decisions like an animal upon its prey, or rushes into action like a torrent from a broken reservoir of water. There are exigencies of life which demand such eruptive outgoes of Volition, but they are rare; and if this kind of Will is characteristic, it surely indicates want of self-control. The true

Will is a constitutional monarch, and is never ruled by mob influences or despotic motives. The Will must control itself, or it is unfit to reign. It may decide quickly and irresistibly, but without violent loosing of its powers. Ordinarily, all violence signifies weakness.

Cure: A healthy tone of the individuality; calmness cultivated, so as to be maintainable in the direst extremity of feeling; a forecasting and vivid realization of the reaction, sure to follow, and which will equal the outburst; a vigorous repression, at the moment of temptation, of all feelings, letting them out in some unimportant side-issue; a determination to recall past experiences, and to profit thereby.

Cultivate the Mood of Reason and Righteousness.

7. *Obstinacy.* We have here an excess of Will as set upon some particular act or state. There are so-called cases of obstinacy which exhibit a curious want of Willpower, but true obstinacy is firmness of Will carried beyond the dictates of reason or right. The obstinate man always believes himself to be right in the matter at hand. His weakness is his refusal to consider. He is willful, not because he is perverse, but because he does not perceive the need for further investigation; the case is with him all settled, and it is rightly settled; he alone is right, all others are obstinate in their difference or their opposition. George the Third and Philip the Second take first rank among incarnations of obstinacy.

Cure: The most minute, as well as the broadest, attention to reasons for or against; greater weight given to the judgment of others; the spirit of concession cultivated; determination to swallow pride and yield to wisdom.

Cultivate the Spirit of Concession.

8. *The Headstrong Will.* The chief characteristic of this disease may be seen in the expression, "I don't care." With neither patience, sentiment nor reason, it rushes the man on to a given act or a line of conduct, unmindful of warning, regardless of self-conviction.

It is not only a case of obstinacy, but of heedlessness as well. It is the Will self-hypnotized by senseless desire. Napoleon on the way to Moscow is the Headstrong Will.

Cure: Cultivation of humility; review of past experiences; resolute heed to the advice of others; elevation into the field of thought of deepest personal convictions; slow, crucifying attention to opposing motives and reasons.

Cultivate the Mood of Reason

9. *Perversity.* The perverse Will is obstinate, but peculiarly set in wrong directions. The Will that is obstinate merely may be fixed by wisdom and right (self-conceived), but perversity of Will shows itself in twisting the dictates of both, notwithstanding the mind's recognition of the same. Thousands of men are perversely willful when they fully know that the course they are pursuing is foolish and injurious. The Will here is strong, but it is used in a manner that is consciously wrong.

Cure: Cultivation of memory as to past experiences, and of imagination as to future; resolution to study previous consequences and to profit by them; determination to force attention upon the opinions of others; persistent and candid examination of one's own character and of the basic principles of human conduct—which are few in number and easily mastered and committed to memory; a condition of mind open to conviction kept steadily before thought; each matter thought out, step by step, mere wish, as much as possible, being put out of the way, and the question, What is right or best? substituted; willingness held fast to give up when convinced.

As an assistance, the mind should change its point of view, get into a new atmosphere of life, and bring about other physical conditions.

Cultivate the Moods of Reason and Righteousness.

10. *Lack of Confidence in Will.*—"This cause is due to a lack of knowledge of the Will, for the reason that a true knowledge of

the will would mean immense confidence in its powers. But, of itself, it is so important that it merits to be put down as a special cause.

"Many will-maladies would disappear if only we trusted in the will. Its native force is so great, its recuperative power is so sure, and its resources so unlimited that it is capable of achieving wonderful results. All that is needed is a firm confidence in it. It is, as we have said, our highest and most perfect faculty. It is the best thing we have, and the most effective weapon that we wield. It alone can develop itself. As we saw, it cannot be trained or perfected from without. It alone can cure its own diseases. The one essential thing is, however, that we should place trust and confidence in it."

Cultivate confidence and belief in your own Will.

11. *In general,* the Will may be said to be diseased when the mind cannot patiently attend; when the mind cannot clearly and persistently exercise memory; when the mind cannot clearly and persistently exercise the imagination; when the mind cannot clearly and persistently exercise the powers of reasoning; when the mind will not call up, and reason in regard to, great moral principles. Because of these failures arise weakness, indecision, fickleness, want of perseverance, violence, obstinacy, headstrong willfulness and perversity.

Cure: Resolute cultivation of the willing-mood, and faithful observance of all exercises suggested in Part III.

CHAPTER V

TRAINING OF THE WILL

The great thing in all education is to make our nervous system our ally instead of our enemy.

For this, we must make automatic and habitual, as early as possible, as many useful actions as we can, and as carefully guard against growing into ways that are likely to be disadvantageous.

In the acquisition of a new habit, or the leaving off of an old one, we must take care to launch ourselves with as strong and decided an initiative as possible.

Never suffer an exception to occur till the new habit is securely rooted in your life.

Seize the very first possible opportunity to act on every resolution you make, and on every emotional prompting you may experience in the direction of the habits you aspire to gain.

—Professor William James

The power of person in Will may be trained and developed, as has been suggested. By this statement is meant, not only that it may be exercised and strengthened by the various agencies of command, encouragement, and instruction in the school-room, but that ability to originate a purposeful action, and to continue a series of actions with an end in view, may be cultivated and disciplined by personal attention thereto, and by specific exercises undertaken by the individual. The *need of such development* and training is evident from the following facts:

"Not unfrequently, a strong volitional power originally exists, but lies dormant for want of being called into exercise, and here it is that judicious training can work its greatest wonders."

In many persons, Willpower is confessedly weak, life being very largely, so to speak, automatic. And in multitudes, the Will exhibits the disorders mentioned in the chapter on "Diseases of the Will".

It is singular that so little would seem to have been written on this important subject, and that the training of the Will should now receive, as it does, such scant attention in modern educational methods. In works on psychology and education, paragraphs may be found here and there indicating the importance of Will-training, but they are curiously deficient in suggestions of methods referring the matter to personal effort.

"The education of the Will is really of far greater importance, as shaping the destiny of the individual, than that of the intellect. Theory and doctrine, and inculcation of laws and propositions, will never of themselves lead to the uniform habit of right action. It is by doing, that we learn to do; by overcoming, that we learn to overcome; by obeying reason and conscience, that we learn to obey; and every right action which we cause to spring out of pure principles, whether by authority, precept or example, will have a greater weight in the formation of character than all the theory in the world."

Education of the mind's powers should not be left to haphazard methods. If the end of education is the evolution of these powers, methods of the direct gymnasium order are in demand. And, as all mental faculties are mutual in interaction, any scientific method which seeks, by specific gymnasium exercises, the development of one faculty, must result in the cultivation of others, whether immediately or remotely related thereto.

Principles in Will-Training

1. Any direct effort to cultivate the perceptive powers must affect the growth of memory, imagination and reason.

2. Any direct effort to cultivate the memory must affect the growth of the perceptive powers, imagination and reason.
3. Any direct effort to cultivate the imagination must affect the growth of the perceptive powers, memory and reason.
4. Any direct effort to cultivate the reasoning powers must affect the perceptive powers, memory and imagination.
5. Any direct effort to cultivate the moral faculties must affect the growth of the perceptive powers, memory, imagination and reason.
6. And any direct effort to cultivate the perceptive powers, memory, imagination, reasoning or moral faculties must affect the growth of the Will.

Yet the application of definite and scientific methods to the discipline and growth of the perceptive powers, the imagination, the memory and the reason seems to be largely wanting in all the schools.

In which school today are classes formed for the education of the power of observation? Where is scientific attention given to the cultivation of the imagination? Which college schedules any definite number of hours to the strengthening and training of the memory? Probably nowhere in the world are there any specific efforts being made to increase and train the power of the Will.

It is the claim of the present work that the Will may be made stronger by the employment of proper methods. And this, (*a*) as a static power through deliberated and intelligent exercises; (*b*) as a dynamic energy continuing through a series of acts by deliberate and intelligent determination that such shall be the case.

Cultivation Of The Will May Be Accomplished:

First, by systematic exercises which shall tend to strengthen it as a faculty.

Activity of the brain reacts upon the particular faculty engaged—to speak more specially, upon the particular brain element engaged—modifying it in some unknown way, and bringing about a subsequent "*physiological disposition*" to act in a particular manner.

Thus, musicians acquire enormous facility in the use of hands and fingers. So, people who have lost their sight are able to picture visible objects independently of external stimulation, having acquired "a disposition so to act through previous exercises *under* external stimulation."

As the seat of the Will is the whole person, so the exercise of willing brings about its own physiological disposition. "The different parts of the brain which are exercised together, acquire in some way a disposition to conjoint action along lines of 'least resistance', that are gradually formed for nervous action by the repeated flow of nerve-energy in certain definite directions."

1. "Lines of least resistance" may be formed by constant action of mind in willing, in certain ways and for certain ends.

"The Cerebrum of man grows to the modes of thought in which it is habitually exercised."

But the development of Will not only involves establishment of facility along the easiest channels, but an *increase in power* within the person as determining to choose motives and to put forth Volitions. The willing-act becomes more facile, and it also becomes stronger. Increase of power is not relative alone; it is equally positive.

"The Will grows by exercise. Each form of its activity becomes more perfect by practice. *And the lower forms of exercise in bodily movement prepare the way, to some extent at least, for the higher exercises.*"

So it is that habits may be voluntarily or unconsciously formed, and old habits may be voluntarily abandoned. All such results involve the Will. Their attainment does not weaken Will, but rather strengthens its application to general conduct. "It is well for our actions to grow habituated to a considerable extent. ... In this way, nerve-energy is economized and the powers of the mind are left free for other matters . . . At the same time . . . much of our life consists in modifying our movements and adapting them to new circumstances. The *growth of Will* implies thus a *two-fold process:* (*a*) the deepening of particular aptitudes and tendencies, that is, the fixing of oft-repeated action in a definite and unvarying form; (*b*) the widening of these active capabilities by a constant variation of old actions, by new adaptations, or special combinations suited to the particular circumstances of the time."

Secondly, the Will may be cultivated by *general improvement of the mind as a whole,* giving it greater force while putting forth Volitions, and larger continuity in a series of Volitions having an end in view, because of increased mental power and wiser treatment of various motives; and this especially if, in all intellectual growth, the purpose of stronger Willpower be kept constantly in mind.

"The Will can never originate any form of mental activity." But it can select among the objects of consciousness, and in thus utilizing the powers of mind can improve the latter. Its efforts to do so will invariably improve itself: by cultivating attention, by shutting out subjects of thought, by developing natural gifts, by instituting correct habits of thinking and of living.

Exercises for a general development of the mind must present a variety of motives for consideration with a view to the act of willing, both for the formation of aptitudes, and for the symmetrical development of the Will as a function. This involves:

1. The *perceptive faculties,* which may be quickened, thus increasing the vividness of motives and inducing Volitions;
2. The *emotions,* the intelligent cultivation of which widens the range of motives and imparts to the mind facility and force in selection of reasons for action;
3. The *imagination,* which represents, according to its strength and scope, various remote and contingent, as

well as immediate, reasons for choice of motives, and adherence to the same;

4. The *deliberative faculty,* which requires cultivation in order to adequately weigh the force and value of motives;
5. The *intuitive faculty,* which, without being able to furnish its reasons, frequently impels or prohibits choice, and may wisely be cultivated by intelligent obedience, but needs strict and constant attention to prevent the reign of impulse. Thus, women are wont to follow intuitions of expediency, and business men are often guided by a similar "feeling" or "judgment". So, also, Socrates possessed what he called his "Daimonion", an inner voice which forbade certain actions, but never affirmatively advised an act or a course of conduct. Such "intuitions" may be searched out and examined for the underlying reasons, and this effort will usually bring to light some hidden cause for the impulse to act or refrain from action.

Thirdly, the Will may be cultivated by *development of the moral character.*

"The greatest man," said Seneca, "is he who chooses right with the most invincible determination."

Self-development involves the moral quality and symmetry of the soul as sustaining relations to its fellows and to Deity. The cultivation of Will in its highest values, therefore, depends upon its exercise in a moral sense. This involves every conscious mental function in action with reference to a moral end. A developed moral consciousness modifies consideration of motives through perception, memory, imagination, reason and "intuition", and increases the force and continuity of that act of the mind by which it constitutes any motive a Sufficient Reason.

Moral development cultivates the Will:

(i) by bringing to the fore truest motives and goals in the conduct of life;

(ii) by presenting in mind for its consideration new motives, and motives of an unfamiliar nature;
(iii) by enabling self to deliberate with greater clearness, forethought and wisdom among all possible motives for action;
(iv) by prohibiting certain acts or lines of conduct, and by destroying injurious habits;
(v) by instituting self-control of the highest order;
(vi) by inspiring a constant search for truth, and obedience thereto;
(vii) by inciting to noblest planes of being and holding before consciousness the great alternatives of human destiny for the ultimate good or evil.

Luther said to Erasmus: "You desire to walk upon eggs without crushing them." The latter replied: "I will not be unfaithful to the cause of Christ, at least so far as the age will permit me." An untruthful Will in a scholar's brain.

"I will go to Worms[2]," shouted Luther, "though devils were combined against me as thick as the tiles upon the housetops!" A Will which might have become disordered or illy developed but for the mighty moral character of the reformer.

All human powers are interdependent and interactive. What has righteousness to do with Willpower? Answer: What has Willpower to do with righteousness? Will makes for righteousness; righteousness makes for Will.

A morally growing life establishes "lines of least resistance", with consequent aptitudes and habits which more or less react upon personal power to will. Above all, at least in this connection, it widens the field of active capabilities and develops new adaptations and tendencies by presenting larger and more varied worlds of motive and conduct, with an ultimate end

---

[2]Worms is a city in Rhineland-Palatinate, in southwest Germany.

having reference to the individual and his relations to others, which end always appeals to the Will, calling it into activity, and so adding to its power.

The *same truth may be reached from a material starting-point.*

The basis of human life is physical. The original ground of impulse in the volitional nature deals with sense-impressions. In a healthy body, these impressions are normal, that is, true. When both body and mind are in a healthy condition, that is to say, are normal and true, they will invariably co-operate, the one with the other.

Instinct co-ordinates with vital chemistry in normal animal life. Such life is true; it is a full realization of itself; it exhibits truth; hence the instincts are right, because the physical basis is right and co-operates with animal intelligence. Instinct and animal intelligence in turn co-operate with the physical nature *to* maintain its normality or truth.

In man, mind ought to co-ordinate similarly with his physical life. Conversely, the physical life ought to co-ordinate with mind. Physical health signifies right, that is, truthful, physical sensations. And truthful, that is, normal, physical sensations tend always to produce right or normal action of mind, just as normal or right action of mind tends to produce good health—truthful physical sensations. When sound mind cooperates with correct sense-impressions, the result is health, normality and truth in the whole man.

Mind is sensation plus perception, plus Will, plus memory, plus imagination, plus reason, plus consciousness—self-consciousness, sub-consciousness, moral consciousness.

If the mind is deficient in any of these respects, the personality is not normal. The end of each function is nothing more nor less than exhibition of truth; perception of things as they are, memory of facts as they have existed, imagination of reality in true relations, conclusions correctly deduced from correct premises and correct observation, convictions based in the actual moral nature of things, sane ideas of self, vigorous action of sub-consciousness, habituating in activities conducive to self-interest, working of objective consciousness for mental freedom. Then there is a perfect co-ordination among all the elements of human nature and character. This co-ordination produces, and it is, health, normality and the truth.

CHAPTER VI

SOME GENERAL RULES

The exercise of the Will, or the lesson of power, is taught in every event. From the child's possession of his several senses up to the hour when he saith, 'Thy will be done!' he is learning the secret, that he can reduce under his Will, not only particular events, but great classes, nay the whole series of events, and so conform all facts to his character.

—Emerson

Part I may be closed with some general rules.

The purpose in suggesting a number of practical rules at this point is twofold: in the first place, the rules furnish examples of what is conceived to be the right use of the Will; and, in the second place, the effort to employ them and fix them in mind will bring into play that fundamentally important factor of our nature, the sub-conscious self. A sea captain wrote to the author in regard to these rules: "I found myself during a stormy passage without effort calling the rules to mind and bringing them into action, and I never got through bad weather so easily."

"There exists in all intellectual endeavor," says Jastrow in "The Subconscious", "a period of incubation, a process in great part sub-conscious, a slow, concealed maturing through absorption of suitable pabulum. Schopenhauer calls it 'unconscious rumination', a chewing over and over again of the cud of thought preparatory to its assimilation with our mental tissue; another speaks of it as the red glow that precedes the white heat. ... We develop by living in an atmosphere congenial to the occupation that we seek, to make our own; by steeping ourselves in the details of the business that is to be our specialty, until the judgment is trained, the assimilation sensitized, the perspective of importance for the special purpose well established, the keenness for useful improvisation brought to an edge. When asked how he came to discover the law of gravitation, Newton is reported to have answered, 'By always thinking about it.' "

First Set

Rules pertinent to the exercise of Will in the conduct of life.

These paragraphs should be studied and thoroughly fixed in mind. They are born of experience, and should be practised daily until they become automatic in the working outfit of character.

1. Be the master of your own Will.
2. When in doubt, do nothing; wait for the light.
3. Cultivate perfect calmness.
4. Never become confusingly excited.
5. Never yield to temper, nor entertain irritation.
6. Make no decision out of temper.
7. If inclined to rashness, cultivate conservatism.
8. If inclined to excessive—injurious—conservatism (experience must decide this), cultivate the prompt and progressive spirit.
9. Decide nothing without deliberation where deliberation is possible.
10. When deliberation is not possible, keep cool. Confusion is mental anarchy; it dethrones the "King".
11. After a decision under such circumstances, entertain no regrets. The regretful mind is an enemy to a good Will. If the mind has held itself with an iron grip and decided on the spur of dire necessity, the gods could do no more.
12. Make no decision without an adequate purpose. Rely upon your own intelligent idea of adequacy.
13. Permit no difficulties to turn you aside from an adequate purpose. Mirabeau called the word "impossible" "that

blockhead word".

14. Never try to make a decision the carrying out of which involves a real impossibility.
15. In the pursuit of an adequate purpose, sift means according to ends, then shift them intelligently. It is folly to tunnel a mountain if you can get a better and cheaper road by going around it. A man in Ohio spent thousands of dollars in laying a roadbed, and abandoned it to purchase another railroad. He should have made sure about the operating road first. But if it is necessary to sink money in a new road in order to compel sale of an old one, that is the thing to do.
16. The best Will is not that which pounds through all circumstances, whether or not, merely for the sake of persistence, but that which "gets there" by taking advantage of shifting conditions. Ends, not means, are the goal of a wise Will.
17. Never lose sight of the main thing in hand.
18. Admit no motive into court which you do not clearly see. A motive is like a would-be soldier; it should undergo medical examination in the nude.
19. Never permit a motive for a decision to tangle up with a motive against. Example: This city is a good business center; but then, you have to earn your money a second time in collecting it. Such a marriage of motives breeds confusion. Compel every motive to stand alone.
20. Remember, that a decision of Will involves a judge and lawyer. You are merely and always the judge. When desire takes the bench and the judge pleads, it is time to adjourn court. You can get a correct "judgment" only by sticking to the bench. In other words, never permit yourself to plead, either with, for or against a motive.
21. In making an important decision, summons the whole mind to this one act. I RESOLVE TO WILL! ATTENTION!

22. Make no decision while the mind is partly occupied with other matters. It is impossible to angle for fish and shoot buffaloes at the same time.
23. Never work at cross-purposes. Set the Will either for one thing or for the other. The man who tries to kill two birds with one stone usually misses both. Where the two birds are taken, a second stone has stolen into the case.
24. Take all the advice that is offered—*then act upon your own judgment.*
25. Never discount your own experience. This is "dollars"—except to the fool. *The chief value of the fool's experience is its worth to others.*
26. Never act upon merely passive resolution. This is weakness. It may be phrased in these words: "I guess I will do so and so." One may say thereto, with Shakespeare, "What a lack-brain is this!" Nothing comes of the lackadaisical Will.
27. If this is the general tone of your Will, stimulate it by imitation of fierce resolution.
28. The first secret of persistence is a good start; the second is a *constant review of motives.*
29. When tempted to discouragement, defer action to a time of sounder mood.
30. Never embark in an enterprise in which you do not thoroughly believe. To do otherwise is to introduce confusion among the judicial powers. If it turns out that your want of faith has been wrong, you have nevertheless kept those *judicial powers on the bench.* That is worth more than the success which you have missed.
31. If you have any settled fears in life, consort with them, resolutely and persistently, *until you know them for liars.*
32. Don't worry! To worry about the past is to dig up a grave; let the corpse lie. To worry about the future is to

dig your own grave; let the undertaker attend to that. The present is the servant of your Will.

33. Never decide an important matter when the mind is confused by sickness. Store this rule in your soul during health; it will stand by you in disease.
34. Never yield a resolution after three o'clock in the afternoon. The morning may bring a better thought.
35. Never make an important decision after three o'clock in the afternoon, nor before ten o'clock in the forenoon. Before ten, you have not "limbered up". After three, you are "unlimbered".

    The two preceding rules are merely for suggestion.
36. Never ignore in deliberation a possible consequence.
37. Insist upon seeing clearly all possible consequences.
38. In *deliberation, consequences* should always be separated from *motives*; in *judgment, motives* should always be considered with reference to *consequences.*
39. Before making a decision, magnify all possible difficulties.
40. After decision, minify every actual difficulty, and throw out of mind every difficulty which seems to be imaginary. Here are some things that are hard to decide; but then, all of life is a taking of chances.
41. If you must take chances, *take those that lean your way.*
42. Learn to emphasize in thought, and to see clearly, remote motives, contingencies and consequences. Be sure that they are not overshadowed by those which are near. Example: I wish to economize in order to secure a home; but at present, I desire a vacation. The home is very remote, while the period of rest is very near and clamorous.
43. In weighing motives, have a care that desire does not tip the scale. "In making an effort to fix our mind on a distant good, or a remote evil we know that we are acting in the direction of our true happiness. Even when

the representation of the immediate result is exerting all its force, and the representation of the distant one is faint and indistinct, we are vaguely aware that the strongest desire lies in this direction. And the resolute direction of attention in this quarter has for its object to secure the greatest good by an adequate process of representation."

44. Never lie to yourself in the consideration of motives and consequences. *If you must lie, practise on other people; they will find you out; but if you continue to lie to yourself, you are a lost fool.*
45. Remember always that the *lie is the dry rot of Will.*
46. Be absolutely genuine and sincere. Yet, withal, this gives you no right to ride rough-shod over neighboring humanity.
47. Never perform an act, nor make a decision, in opposition to what Socrates called his "Daimonion"—the inner voice that whispers, "Better not!"
48. When you write to an enemy a letter in which you scorch his soul, be happy—but do not mail it until tomorrow. You will then see that you have written too much. Condense it by half—but do not mail it until tomorrow. It will keep. Do not destroy it. It is a good letter. Tomorrow you will again condense it. When you can write a brief, plain, but courteous letter, in which you reveal good breeding and disclose reticence, do so, and instantly mail it, grateful for common sense.
49. Never resolve upon an act which will, or may injure other people, or injure yourself.
50. *Measure motives by your noblest selfhood.*
51. Dismiss without consideration motives or actions which you clearly recognize to be contrary to your best instincts.
52. In all conflicts between duty and pleasure, give duty the

benefit of the doubt.

53. Never act contrary to your clearest judgment. Others may be right; but, in the long run, better is mistake in your own judgment than right on the judgment of others. *Do not abdicate the throne.*
54. Cultivate as a permanent habit of mind the positive Mood of willing.
55. Never will to be an imitator or a follower. You can so will unconsciously; therefore, resolve to lead and to invent and move out on new lines.

It is impossible to deliberate over every detail of conduct. Hence, life must become habituated to right general principles. "A force endowed with intelligence, capable of forming purposes and pursuing self-chosen ends, may neglect those rules of action which alone can guide it safely, and thus at last wholly miss the natural ends of its being. To such a being, eternal vigilance would be the price of liberty."

Second Set

Rules having reference to the Moods of mind.

I. *The Mood of Feeling*
   1. Never yield to the Mood of Feeling without scrutinizing it closely.
   2. In cultivating this Mood, be sure that it is wholly free from wrong desire, fear, hate, prejudice, jealousy, anger, revenge, nervous disorders, mental depression, misconceptions and partial views.
   3. At no time, permit this Mood to explode in impulse.
   4. Keep the Mood constantly at a high, but rational and controlled, pitch or tone.

II. *The Mood of Energy*
   1. Seek every opportunity to intensify consciousness of the

determined Will.
2. Maintain the resolute sense of the emphatic personality.
3. Keep the Mood under firm control.
4. Permit no explosion without deliberate decision and adequate cause.
5. Bring this Mood to all activities.
6. Hold the eye of energy upon life's ultimate goal.

III. *The Mood of Decision*
1. Precede all decision by deliberation.
2. Cultivate decision in so-called unimportants.
3. Endeavor constantly to reduce the time expended in arriving at decision. Do everything as swiftly as possible.
4. Never defer decided action. Go immediately into the business determined upon.
5. Always conjoin with this Mood that of energy.

IV. *The Mood of Continuity*
1. Count the cost.
2. Repeat constantly the resolution involved.
3. Do not brood over difficulties.
4. Keep the goal in sight.
5. In all continuous effort hold to the fore the Mood of utmost energy, and cause decision to act like a trip-hammer incessantly on the purposed business.
6. Regard each step or stage as a goal in itself. Act by act—the thing is done!

V. *The Moods of Understanding and Reason*
1. Know, first, what the matter proposed involves.
2. Know, secondly, what defeat means.
3. Know, thirdly, what success signifies.
4. Understand your own weakness.
5. Understand your own powers.
6. Thoroughly understand *how* to proceed.
7. Become acquainted with all details connected with an

undertaking, and with the reasons for one method of procedure or another.

VI. *The Mood of Righteousness*

1. Have perfect faith in yourself.
2. Have faith in men.
3. Be honest—absolutely honest—with yourself.
4. Permit nothing in self to hoodwink judgment.
5. Put yourself always in the other man's shoes.
6. Examine all moral traditions.
7. Reject nothing because it is old.
8. Approve nothing because it is new.
9. Settle no question by expediency.
10. Seek all possible light.
11. Live up to all light possessed.
12. Follow your best instincts.
13. Try your ideas by the opinions of others.
14. Surrender to all good and *wise* impulses.
15. *Love truth supremely.*
16. Be as anxious to discover duty as you ought to be to perform it when discovered.

The following remarkable paragraph, by John Stuart Mill, almost epitomizes the right use of Willpower:

"He who chooses his plan for himself, employs all his faculties. He must use *observation* to see, *reasoning* and *judgment* to foresee, *activity* to gather materials for *decision, discrimination* to decide, and when he has decided, *firmness* and *self-control* to hold to his deliberate decision. And these qualities he requires and exercises exactly in proportion as the part of his conduct which he determines according to his own judgment and feeling is a large one. It is possible that he might be guided in some good path, and kept out of harm's way, without any of these things. But what will be his comparative worth as a human being? It really is of importance not only what men do, but also what manner of men they are that do it. Among the works of man, which human life is rightly employed in perfecting and beautifying, the first in importance surely is man himself."

But the work of this chapter will not be finished so long as dependence is placed on the objective self alone. There is a deeper self which must be trained to accept and act on the rules above suggested. It is a mistake to expect self-development from external activities exclusively. If you go over the rules until they are thoroughly imbedded in the sub-conscious phases of your mind, they will then "germinate", so to speak, and in time become "second nature". In the meantime, it will be advisable to affirm mentally somewhat as follows: "I am absorbing these principles of conduct, and in so doing am affirming that the moods indicated are surely becoming mine, actual factors in my everyday life."

For remember, you cannot find reality, truth, life, a universe, by going forever outside of self nor by gazing into some imaginary sky. So far as you are concerned, none of these things exist save as each is given existence within your selfhood. The Universe passes solemnly through every growing soul from the region of the ungrasped and below the ordinary consciousness. No knowledge comes from upper airs—though half the reality of any knowledge lies there because every individual centers Infinite Existence—but all emerges from the under realm of the unknown in consciousness. No possession is yours until it has swept up from the lower inner fields of life.

Stand, therefore, for the objective life, of course, but always as well for the inner existence which allies you with all worlds. If, taking the outer life as it comes, you will for long affirm that your deeper self is also in relation with all right things and growing because of that relation, you will in this way realize the remarkable quotation from Mill. Otherwise, it is nothing better than commonplace school instruction.

PART II

THE WILL AND SENSE-CULTURE

CHAPTER VII

SUGGESTIONS FOR PRACTICE

Nature is often hidden, sometimes overcome, seldom extinguished. He that seeketh victory over his nature, let him not set himself too great nor too small tasks; for the first will make him dejected by often failings, and the second will make him a small proceeder, though by often prevailings. Let not a man force a habit upon himself with a perpetual continuance, but with some intermission. For both the pause reenforceth the new onset; and if a man that is not perfect be ever in practice, he shall as well practice his errors as his abilities, and induce one habit of both. And there is no means to help this but by seasonable intermissions.

—Lord Bacon

Should the exercises given in this division of our work, Part II, seem unin essential or tedious, you are invited to remember that, as Josiah Royce has said (in "Outlines of Psychology"): "The development and support of mental activities of every grade is dependent upon the constant and proper use of the sense organs. Every cultivation of even the highest inner life involves a cultivation of the sense organs."

But observe: "The life of the senses does not constitute a sort of lower life, over against which the higher intellectual, emotional and voluntary life stands, as a markedly contrasted region relatively independent of the other, and ideally capable of a certain divorce from it. On the contrary, sensory experience plays its part, and its essential part, in the very highest of our spiritual existence. When we wish to cultivate processes of abstract thinking, our devices must, therefore, include a fitting plan for the cultivation of the senses, and must not plan to exclude sense experience as such, but only to select among sensory experiences those that will prove useful for a purpose."

We are now prepared for the actual work of Will culture in Physical Regime. The present chapter is preliminary yet eminently practical, and it should not only be carefully read but thoroughly studied until its suggestions are deeply grounded in daily life.

At this point, *certain principles* appear which form the basis of all Physical Regime.

First Principle

Continuous and intelligent thought on the growth of any mental power, with exercises carried on to that end, exerts a developing influence upon the function itself. In the case of the Will, this would follow without systematic practise, but regulated exercise tends to hold attention to the desired goal and to increase the power of the idea of Will-culture. The value of the abiding thought, "I resolve to acquire a strong and well-trained Will!" can scarcely be overstated.

Second Principle

Exercises involving one department of body or mind will exert various beneficial influences:

Of the body, on other parts of the body;
Of the body, on various powers of the mind;
Of the mind, on other powers of the mind;
Of the mind, on various functions and organs of the body.

An illustration of the general law may be seen in the increased grip-power of one hand caused by daily practise with the other. Thus, Professor E.W. Scripture, in "Thinking, Willing, Doing", remarks:

"It is incredible to me how in the face of our general experience of gymnasium work some writers can assert that practise makes no change in the greatest possible effort. At any rate, in experiments made under my direction, the change could be traced day by day.

"Curiously enough, this increase of force is not confined to the particular act. In the experiments referred to, the greatest possible effort in gripping was made on the first day with the left hand singly and then with the right hand, ten times each. The records were: for the left, fifteen pounds, for the right, fifteen pounds. Thereafter, the right hand alone was practised nearly every day for eleven days, while the left hand was not used. The right hand gained steadily day by day; on the twelfth day, it recorded a grip of twenty-five pounds. The left hand recorded on the same day a grip of twenty-one pounds. Thus, the left hand had gained six pounds, or more than one-third, by practise of the other hand."

In practise seeking development of Will, what is true of the hands will be true of mental powers. Indeed, *steadfast, purposeful exercise of physical powers in general will develop power of Will.* The same writer goes on to say on this point:

"A great deal has been said of the relation of physical exercise to Willpower. I think that what I have said sufficiently explains how we can use the force of an act as an index of Willpower. It is unquestionable that gymnastic exercises increase the force of act. The conclusion seems clear; the force of Will for those particular acts must be increased. It has often been noticed that an act will grow steadily stronger although not the slightest change can be seen in the muscle.

"Of course I do not say that the developed muscle does not give a greater result for the same impulse than the undeveloped one; but I do claim that much of the increase or decrease of strength is due to a change in Willpower. For example, no one would say that Sandow, the strong man, has a more powerful

Will than anybody else. But Sandow's strength varies continually, and, although part of this variation may be due to changes in the muscles, a large portion is due to a change in force of Will. When Sandow is weak, make him angry, and note the result."

Third Principle

Lower forms of exercise in bodily movement prepare the way for higher exercises. "All the higher actions of life depend on the attainment of a general control of the bodily organs." This is true even when such control is left to haphazard methods. It is immeasurably truer when control is intelligently sought. "Consequently," in the highest sense, "the exercising of these capabilities involves a rudimentary," and a very complete "training of the Will, for a definite reaction on the Will itself is absolutely certain."

Fourth Principle

Intelligent work in Will-culture must begin with perception. Perception precedes mental growth. The senses are our common miners for raw material of mental life. Yet how few people adequately attend to sensation or intelligently employ their own senses! Strange as it may seem, here is a large *terra incognita.* One of the chief differences among men is the matter of vision. By vision is meant the ability to see, hear and feel reality. Some people perceive a great deal on the surface of things; others catch but little even here. Some perceive not only the superficial aspects of reality, but also its inner contents; others, again, discover neither the surface of things nor their hidden meaning. Eyes, ears, nerves they have; but they see not, hear not, feel not. To such people, a strong Willpower is a stranger. They are governed largely by caprice.

The *first requisite,* then, *of Will-growth,* is *observation.* The mind must learn to see things as they are, to hear things as they are, to feel things as they are.

"Eyes and No-eyes journeyed together," says the author just quoted. "No-eyes saw only what thrust itself upon him; Eyes was on the watch for everything. Eyes used the *fundamental method of all knowledge—observation, or watching.*

"This is the first lesson to be learned—the art of watching. Most of us went to school before this art was cultivated, and, alas! most of the children still go to schools of the same kind. There are proper ways of learning to watch, but the usual object lessons in school result in just the opposite. We, however, cannot go a step further till we have learned how to watch."

Hence, the watchword all along must be ATTENTION! The Will must begin its work by resolving upon persistent ATTENTION. To the various operations of the senses, WILL must mightily attend! In all exercises, the watchword must never be forgotten: ATTENTION! But attention for what purpose? For one sole purpose—*Willpower!* The commanding formula, then, is—"I RESOLVE TO WILL! ATTENTION!"

Fifth Principle

Systematic exercise, with the power of Will constantly kept in mind as a goal never to be yielded, *develops the Will-habit.* Hence the value of persistence. Practise develops persistence; persistence perfects practise. Emerson said truly:

"The second substitute for temperament is drill, the power of use and routine. The hack is a better roadster than the Arab barb. At West Point, Colonel Buford, the Chief Engineer, pounding with a hammer on the trunnions[3] of a cannon, until he broke them off. He fired a piece of ordnance some hundred times in

[3]Trunnions is either of the two cylindrical projections on a cannon, one on each side for supporting the cannon on its carriage.

swift succession, until it burst. Now, which stroke broke the trunnion? Every stroke. Which blast burst the piece? Every blast. '*Diligence passe sens,*' Henry VIII was wont to say, or, 'Great is drill.' Practice is nine-tenths. Six hours every day at the piano, only to give facility of touch; six hours a day at painting, only to give command of the odious materials, oil, ochres, and brushes. The masters say that they know a master in music, only by seeing the pose of the hands on the keys—so difficult and vital an act is the command of the instrument. To have learned the use of the tools, by thousands of manipulations; to have learned the arts of reckoning, by endless adding and dividing, is the power of the mechanic and the clerk."

"Not only men," says Thomas Reid, the English Philosopher, "but children, idiots, and brutes, acquire by habit many perceptions which they had not originally. Almost every employment in life hath perceptions of this kind that are peculiar to it. The shepherd knows every sheep of his flock, as we do our acquaintance, and can pick them out of another flock one by one. The butcher knows by sight the weight and quality of his beeves and sheep before they are killed. The farmer perceives by his eye very nearly the quantity of hay in a rick or corn in a heap. The sailor sees the burden, the build, and the distance of a ship at sea, while she is a great way off. Every man accustomed to writing, distinguishes acquaintances by their handwriting, as he does by their faces. In a word, acquired perception is very different in different persons, according to the diversity of objects about which they are employed, *and the application they bestow in observing them.*"

All such acquired powers are the results of long-continued practise. And back of them lies the persistent Will. In the most of such and similar instances, no great amount of Will is required at any one time; they are rather outcomes of steady application to the thing in hand.

Thus, unfailing attention to the exercises here to follow, with the idea of power of Will constantly in mind, will impart facility as regards the directions given, and in turn will develop the controlling faculty of mind to an astonishing degree.

But this work, to be successful, must be conducted with labor and patience. Think not to acquire a great Will without toil. Nor imagine that such a boon can come of a month's training or of spasmodic effort. There is but one way to get a good Will; to will to will, and to carry out that will with unflinching perseverance.

The insane are sometimes able, *for a purpose,* to "wind themselves up", and act like the sanest, by a supreme effort of Will. If the present book costs you many months of endeavor, it will "wind up" the Will to great power and persistence, and will justify all time and toil.

Sixth Principle

The value of drill depends largely upon system. This requires not only regular labor, but regular rest-periods as well.

In the ten-day exercises, continue five days, then rest—preferably Saturday and Sunday.

From first to last, cultivate and sustain the Mood of Will. Put the Will at the fore. Here alone is our *ne plus ultra!*

Finally, in order that the principles involved may become an intelligent part of the system carried out, the following suggestions applicable to the Physical and Mental Regimes should be thoroughly worked into the student's mind as to:

First.—*In Regard to Perception.*

1. Keep the perceptive powers always at their best: eyes, ears, smell, taste, touch, nerves.
2. Attend to the *consciousness* of each sense.
3. *Observe frequent and regular periods of rest.* The law that "voluntary attention comes only in beats", requires this rule.

4. With attainment of facility, invent new methods of practise.
5. Carry the idea involved in practise into all your life.
6. While habituated actions that are not *naturally* automatic are certainly voluntary, the presence of *conscious* Will should be maintained as much as possible in all such activities. Example: in piano playing, hold the mind consciously to every movement.
7. Continue the practise of the perceptive powers until the greatest willing power has been acquired.

Secondly.—*In Regard to Memory.*

1. If the memory is weak all round, resolve to strengthen it.
2. Seek to discover the peculiarities of your own memory. Then make the most of it.
3. If the memory is weak in some particulars, but strong in others, cultivate it especially where weak, and compel it where strong to assist in this effort.
4. Subordinate the verbal memory to that of principles.
5. Give memory for principles a good foundation in memorized facts, dates, etc.
6. Rely resolutely upon the ability of your memory to do your bidding.
7. Frequently review all work of the memory with great Willpower.
8. Make use, as often as possible, in conversation and writing, and in public speaking, of all the acquirements of memory.
9. Always put the Will into the effort to remember.
10. Arrange materials by association. Then systematize and associate memory's possessions.
11. Resolve to acquire a perfect memory.
12. Abstain from all use of tobacco and alcohol.
13. Put no reliance in mnemonics, or any arbitrary "helps",

but employ natural laws of association, such as:
"Contiguity...Horse and rider.
Contrast...Light and dark.
Resemblance...Grant and Sherman.
Cause and effect...Vice and misery.
Whole and parts...United States and New York.
Genus and species...Dog and greyhound.
Sign and thing signified...Cross and Catholic faith."

Thirdly.—*In Regard to Imagination.*

1. Do not indulge in reverie.
2. Abstain from all evil imaginations.
3. Deal, in the imagination, with facts and essential reality alone.
4. Fill the mind with wholly admirable material.
5. Put the Will-sense into the imagination.
6. Make the imagination a *conscious* and *intelligent* instrument. Use it for practical purposes.
7. Beware of the "squint" brain. Look at things squarely and without prejudice.
8. Do not fall in love with the wonderful for its own sake.
9. Do not permit the imagination to dwell upon any one thing, nor upon any one quarter of thought or life, for long at one time.
10. Provide for the imagination the greatest variety of material.
11. Rigidly exclude from the realm of fancy all imaginary ills, and especially misconceptions about men or reality. Guard against deception here.

Fourthly.—*In Regard to Self-perception,*

1. Do not suffer the mind to become morbid.
2. Subject the testimony of the senses and of the mind to the closest scrutiny of reason.

3. Maintain in all seasons the healthy mood. Keep up your supply of ozone.
4. Live among wholesome people.
5. Companion only with large and vigorous truths.
6. Thrust the Will into all perception of self. Banish the dream-mood. Turn a hurricane in on hallucinations.
7. Become familiar with self-perception in every phase: seeing, hearing, smelling, tasting, touching, muscular consciousness, nerve-testimony; feeling, memory, imagination, reason, Will, moral states. Be absolute master here.

Fifthly.—*In Regard to Self-control.*

1. Habituate normal and right actions.
2. Eliminate eccentricities.
3. Study and overcome your personal faults.
4. Destroy immoral, injurious and obnoxious habits.
5. Expend no unnecessary amount of force in legitimate effort, and none at all in illegitimate effort.
6. Welcome criticism; but sift it thoroughly, and then act upon results.
7. Never gratify impulse or desire if either offers a single chance of permanent injury to the *highest tone* of mind.
8. When about to lose self-control, anticipate consequences, and foresee especially what you may be required to do in order to regain position.
9. Make discipline an ally, not an enemy.
10. Believe mightily in yourself.
11. Unite belief in self with faith in man.
12. Keep the loftiest ideals fresh in thought.
13. Never, for an instant, lose consciousness of self as a willing center of power.

Seventh Principle

"There is nothing which tends so much to the success of a volitional effort as a confident expectation of its success."

Cultivate, therefore, the Mood of Expectancy.

There are underlying, scientifically demonstrated truths of tremendous import in this connection. Space does not allow going into a lengthy explanation. But the idea is: The positive mind that DEMANDS, mentally, the things it wants, is far more likely to get them than the cringing, shrinking, negative state of mind. Some rules in this connection follow:

1. Be sure the intended effort is one within the possibility of your powers to carry through.
2. If it is possible to choose the time of applying the final effort, select a period when you are at your best, physically and mentally.
3. Impress upon your mind, over and over again, the demand that you simply MUST win. Scout and ridicule the little flickering thoughts that pipe up: "*There's a big possibility that you won't get it.*"
4. Mentally demand, over and over, and with intensest vigor of thought, that you shall and will get what you seek. Say: "I DEMAND health. I DEMAND luxuries. I DEMAND better things in life. I simply MUST have them. I DEMAND the universal forces to bring into my career the values I seek. I DEMAND THEM!"

If this seems far-fetched—just bear in mind that you are using that positive state of mind which is exactly the opposite of the cringing, timid condition which you know is the sort that gets "kicked aside". If the negative phases of mind gets what it expects (kicks, drudgery, slights, life's dregs), then beyond any question the POSITIVE mind can get the big things it demands.

CHAPTER VIII

EXERCISES FOR THE EYE

It is estimated that the human eye is capable of distinguishing 100,000 different colors, or hues, and twenty shades or tints of each hue, making a total of 2,000,000 color sensations which may be discriminated. If we considered the infinite variations in the color of earth, of plants and their blossoms, of clouds, in fact of all natural objects, such an estimate as this hardly seems excessive.

—D. Harold Wilson

Theory of this Chapter

The whole mind in the eye;
The eye an index of white honesty[4]*;*
The straight line the path of power.

Epictetus said: "Did God give the eyes for nothing? And was it for nothing that He mingled in them a spirit of such *might and cunning* as to reach a long way off and receive the impression of visible forms—a messenger so swift and faithful? Was it for nothing that He gave the intervening air such efficacy, and made it elastic, so that being, in a manner *strained,* our vision should traverse it? Was it for nothing that He made Light, without which there were no benefit of any other thing?"

[4]'White honesty' is a term used by the author, who also referred to life as 'white life', or divine life, in other books.

Preliminary

The eye exists for the supreme power of Will.

Eye, ether, light, are ministers to the soul. The eye may be brightened in its gaze by energetic summonsing of consciousness. Emotions of joy, fear, hate, love, desire, aversion, illustrate this deepening influence of energy within. These emotions may be simulated, as on the stage, at the imperious call of Will. If so, one may acquire a keen eye, without the assistance of these feelings, by sheer and persistent resolution.

The present chapter is to deal with the eye. It may, nevertheless, be here said that it partakes of a law which obtains with all the organs of sense: "*A process set up anywhere in the centers reverberates everywhere, and in some way or other affects the organism throughout.*"

Effort at Will-growth by means of exercise of the senses will bring this law into action. Each particular variety of practice will more or less affect the whole man—that is, the central Will.

Vision, hearing, taste, smell and touch depend upon certain stimulations from without—as mechanical (touch), molecular (taste and smell), physical (sight, hearing), muscular (muscle sense), vital (sense of life).

But at times, the required stimulation may arise within the nervous system. Examples: In referring to certain hallucinations, a Boston physician said, "The cerebral processes by which vision is produced may not only be started in the brain itself, but when so started, they are identical with those set going by an objective stimulus in the ordinary way."

Professor Sully says: "A man who has lost his sight may be able to picture visible objects. The brain is now able to act *independently* of external stimulation, having acquired a disposition so to act through previous exercises *under* external stimulation." But it could not picture objects it had never seen.

Two remarks may now be made:

The Will has power to concentrate energy upon a given point in the organism. "By fixing the attention upon certain parts of the body the blood may be directed to these parts." A strong attention directed to the eye enriches its various elements. "In looking attentively at anything, the various ganglia in which the optic nerve is rooted are richly supplied with blood, and the end organs of vision and the eye muscles are vigorously innervated."

Similarly, attention increases the supply of nervous force at the point where Will is focused.

Vision is intensified by attention, which induces a degree of muscular effort:—physical energy from within directed to appropriate muscles. "In all close attention, there is a feeling of *tension or strain* which appears to indicate muscular effort. As Fechner says, in looking steadfastly this feeling is referred to the eye; in listening closely, to the ear; in trying to 'to think' or recollect, to the head or brain."

"Thus it is presumable that when we attend to a visible object, a stream of (nerve-) energy flows downward from the motor centers, partly in the direction of the muscles, and more particularly the ocular muscles which move the eye, and partly in that of the sensory center which is concerned in the reception of nervous impressions."

If a person tries to grip the hand of a paralyzed arm, he cannot, but muscular effort will manifest in some part of his body. Energy has been expended.

In other words, "the stimuli that excite the nervous force or irritability are of two kinds, physical and mental. Physical stimuli embrace all external excitants of whatever nature— light, heat, sound, odor, and every variety of chemical, mechanical, and galvanic irritant. *Mental stimuli result from the exercise of the Will and thought.*"

The Will is thus the power back of vision.

Professor James cites the case of a girl, born without arms or legs, who "came as quickly to a right judgment of the size and distance of visible objects as her brothers and sisters, although she had no use of hands."

Many children have the power of calling up "queer" forms in the darkness.

Cases like the following are not altogether rare: "A man in the Greek island of Hydra was accustomed to take his post every day for thirty years on the summit of the island, and look out for the approach of vessels; and although there were over three hundred sail belonging to the island, he would tell the name of each one as she approached with unerring certainty, while she was still at such a distance as to present to a common eye only a confused white blur upon the clear horizon." The long practice which resulted in this ability involved volitional acts.

The greater the Will (with a good eye), the greater our capacity for correct vision.

As exercise with vision improves the eye, so such exercise augments the flow of energy to the appropriate muscles and nerve-centers connected with sight.

Hence, conversely, all right exercises with the eyes tend to growth of that power which controls the eyes—the Will—provided they are carried on with that end held intensely in view.

In the following practice, therefore, the mind must take on energy, and it must energetically, *attend* to the thing in hand by the whole of itself, excluding all other elements of perception. This will at first be difficult; as in the case of any muscular or nervous exertion. But to him who constantly declares, "I RESOLVE TO WILL! ATTENTION!" perfect power of continued and exclusive concentration comes at last to be second nature.

"*The culminating point in education is the power to attend to things that are in themselves indifferent, by arousing an artificial feeling of interest.*"

Hence, in the exercises that follow, the Mood or feeling of Will should be kept strongly in mind.

Regimes

Exercise No. 1. Select an object for attention, in the room, or out of doors, say, a chair or a tree. Gaze at this object attentively, persistently, steadily. Do not strain the eyes; use them naturally. Now, note the object's size. Estimate this. Observe its distance from yourself, and from other objects around it. Note its shape. Determine how it differs in shape from other things near it. Clearly note its color. Does it in this harmonize with its surroundings? If so, how? If not, in what respect. Make out its material. How was it made? What is its true purpose? Is it serving that purpose? Could it in any way be improved? How might this improvement be brought about?

In seeking the above information, *hold the mind rigidly to its task.* It will be hard at first; but persistence in the exercise will ultimately secure ease and swiftness.

Now, without looking further at the object, write out all results as nearly as you can remember.

Repeat this exercise for ten days, resting two days, one of which should be Sunday, with the same object, and on the tenth day, look at the object and observe improvement.

Always keep the Will-idea in mind.

Exercise No. 2. At a moderate gait, pass once through or around a room, observing, quickly and attentively, as many objects as possible. Now, closing the door so as to shut out the room, write down the names of all articles which you remember at that time to have seen. Depend upon your memory, not your knowledge.

Repeat this exercise for ten days with rest, as above, and on the tenth observe improvement.

Finally, go into the room and note carefully every object which you have not discovered. Estimate the percentage of your failures.

Exercise No. 3. Procure twenty-five or thirty marbles, of medium size. Let eight or ten be red, eight or ten yellow, eight or ten white. Place them in an open box and thoroughly mingle the colors. Now, seize one handful, with right and left hand at once, and let the marbles roll out together onto a covered surface, of a table or the floor. When they are at rest, glance once at the lot, and, turning away, write the number, as you recall (do not guess) for each color.

Repeat this exercise for ten days, with rest, and on the tenth day, estimate your improvement.

Exercise No. 4. Procure fifty pieces of cardboard, two inches square, each having one letter printed upon it in plain, good-sized type. Place them all, scattered, letters down, upon a table. Take in one hand ten of these squares, face down, and throw, face up, all at once, but so as to separate them, upon the table. Now, look at them sharply one instant. Then turn away, and write down the letters recalled. Immediately repeat this exercise with ten other cards. Immediately repeat with ten other cards. Repeat these three exercises for ten days, with rest, and on the tenth day, note improvement for each successive corresponding throw over first.

The above exercises should all be practised each day, for ten days, at least. They may be continued indefinitely with profit, both to attention and to the Will. But the rest periods must be observed.

Exercise No. 5. Let the eyes be wide open, but not disagreeably distended. The gaze should now be directed straight in front, with every power of attention alert. Try to observe, without turning the eyes a hair's breadth, all objects in the field of vision, while gazing for ten seconds, determined by slow counting. Write out the names of all objects recalled. Depend upon memory, not knowledge.

Repeat the exercise ten days, with rest, as above, always from the same position, looking in the same direction, to preserve the same exercise, and on the tenth day, note the improvement.

Exercise No. 6. Repeat the above exercise in all respects except that the position and field of vision of each day is to be different from those preceding, and on the tenth day, note the improvement.

Observe: Counting off the seconds is a slower process than is ordinarily supposed. The speed with which one must count in order to pronounce "sixty" at the end of a minute may be easily noted by counting while following with the eyes the second-hand of a watch as it moves once around the minute-circle.

Exercise No. 7. Gaze steadily, winking naturally, at some object not very far away, say, at ten or sixty feet. Keep the mind intently upon the object. Count sixty to a minute while so gazing intently and observingly. Now, shut the eyes, and strive to call up a mental image of the object.

With some people, the image may be as vividly denned as the real object. With most, probably, it will not be so vivid. Look up that word "vivid". Write a description of the image, whether clear or indistinct, with all parts mentally seen. Do not help the writing by looking a second time at the object; trust the image. Repeat this exercise on ten different objects on the same day. Repeat these exercises for ten days, with rest, as above, making and marking records each day, and on the tenth day note the improvement.

Although the time set for practise is ten days, the exercises may be profitably continued for any length of time.

Remember: the purpose here is to learn to see things as they are, and to impress them upon the mind. Great improvement, both in distinctness of vision and in details of single mental objects may thus be made as practise goes on. The essential thing, now, is patience and persistence. Whether the mental image may be cultivated so that the mental objects shall assume the electric or sunlit tone, seems doubtful. But, within certain limits, the eye of the soul will come to see more and more clearly as persistent endeavor continues. Especially will this be the case if the soul steadfastly wills that it be so.

The value of the end sought—clear perception—connects ultimately with the consideration of motives. This requires that things shall be seen as they actually are, that outcomes or consequences shall be vividly noted, in themselves individually and as comprehended in groups, in order that their full effect upon mind may be felt, and that adequate comparison among motives may be instituted. These exercises cultivate eye-perception, memory, mental vision and self-control. The end of all is the developed Will.

Exercise No. 8. Lastly, the eye may be trained to directness of gaze. Some eyes never look into other eyes steadily, but glance and shift from eye to object, here and there, without purpose or gain. Some public speakers never look squarely into the faces of their auditors, but gaze either up at the ceiling or down to the floor, or roam over all their hearers, seeing none. One of the subtlest elements of inspiration is thus missed—the face, mouth, eyes, attitude of eager humanity. As a rule, a large element in successful personal address lies in the eye. Directness of gaze is psychological winner. The straightforward, frank eye is a power wherever it is seen—on the street, in the store, at the social gathering, on the rostrum.

The might of a good eye can be cultivated. In order to this, mind must be put into the "windows of the soul". What men get out of life and nature depends upon the amount of mind that can be put into the look. If reality is to be possessed, the mind must come forward and take it "by force". The soul in the eye means power with men. Cultivate, therefore, with every person met, the habit of the direct and steady look. Do not stare. Look at people full in the eyes. The soul must always be in the eye for this exercise. Let the gaze be open, frank, friendly. And remember, that the vacant stare is a sign of idiocy, and in the domain of Will is ruled out.

Exercise No. 9. Gaze steadily, but winking naturally, at a small spot on the wall of a room, at eight or ten feet away. *Do not strain the eyes.* Count fifty while so gazing. Keep mind wholly on the thought: *The Direct Eye.* Put at the back of that thought the Mood of a strong Will: "I WILL! I AM FORCING WILL INTO THE EYE."

Repeat this exercise ten times for ten days, with rest, as above, adding each day to the count fifty, twenty counts; thus, first day, fifty; second day, seventy; third day, ninety; etc.

Exercise No. 10. A dull gaze is akin to the vacant stare. The steady, direct look ought to be bright and full of energy. The energy of the eye's regard may be developed, and with profit, if the soul behind it is honest.

Gaze at any object in the room nearby, steadily, but naturally, that is permitting the eyes to wink as they will. Put the whole soul into the eyes. Observe, *the soul is to be put into the eyes,* not into or upon the object. And do not look at the nose; look at the object, but bring consciousness forward to its windows. Summon your entire energy to the act of looking. Do this repeatedly, resting properly, and never permitting the eyes to grow weary or to be strained.

Now, think of, and simulate, some emotion, and try to look that feeling with great power. Examples: Intense interest—Throw delighted attention into the eyes. Deep joy—Assume a genuine joyful feeling and expression. Avoid the grinning mimicry of the clown. Fierce hate —Blaze a look at the ink-stand sufficient to annihilate its black shape. Thus with all emotions of the soul.

Repeat these exercises daily for months. It is really worthwhile. After a time, you will discover that you are the possessor of a good eye, and that your power of Will has grown correspondingly.

CHAPTER IX

EXERCISES FOR THE EAR

I had an opportunity of repeatedly observing the peculiar manner in which he (Dr Saunderson) arranged his ideas and acquired his information. Whenever he was introduced into company, I remarked that he continued some time silent. The sound directed him to judge of the dimensions of the room, and the different voices of the number of persons that were present. His distinction in these respects was very accurate, and his memory so retentive that he was seldom mistaken. I have known him instantly to recognize a person on first hearing him, though more than two years had elapsed since the time of their meeting.

—"Manchester Philosophical Memoirs"

Theory of this Chapter

The discriminating mind in the ear;
The mind master of hearing;
Direct improvement of Will through willed employment of this sense.

"Well, early in autumn, a first winter-warning,
When the stag had to break with his foot, of a morning,
A drinking-hole out of the fresh, tender ice,
That covered the pond till the sun, in a trice,
Loosening it, let out a ripple of gold,
And another and another, and faster,
Till, dimpling to blindness, the wide water rolled."

Preliminary

If you can see that picture from Browning, you probably can hear the sounds that go with it.

Natural defects aside, one good sense-power assists all the senses. When attention of the eye begins, the ear often follows. Here is the first communion. Hence three questions arise:

Do you *hear*? Do you hear *correctly*? Do you hear *what you wish to hear*?

Sounds are produced by vibrations in the atmosphere. The human ear is limited in its ability to respond to these vibrations. Within such natural limits, the more sounds one can make out, the better one's hearing. Loss of sounds is due to defects of ear and abstraction of the mind.

If one hears all noises does one necessarily hear correctly? That is, is the soul always in the ear? To distinguish tone, quality, direction, etc., of sounds? Is any difference obtaining in this respect due to endowment or education? Or both? Probably the latter is true. The value of exercises, therefore, to train the ear—to unfold latent powers—is evident.

Hearing what one wishes to hear may involve exclusion: one desires to shut out a noise. Or inclusion: one wishes to enjoy, truly, deeply, certain sounds, harmonies, music. All depends, now, on the soul. The nervous person hears everything. The dull person hears little.

Hearing may be shut out by Will. The door is closed to a certain sound. Hearing may be rendered more acute by Will. "Listen! A far-off bird is singing!" "Sh! A burglar is in the house!" Education in correctness of ear is preeminently a matter of Will—but of the persistent Will. The control of the ear exhibits some of the highest phases of self-direction. The educated soul now mounts up on wings through the realm of harmony.

But feeling, thought, imagination, are here the masters. To hear in the best sense involves the soul. Other things being equal, the largest soul hears most, most correctly, and with greatest powers of appreciation and appropriation.

The purpose of the exercises that follow is, as with those for the eye, development of ability to consider motives through discipline of attention, and thus the growth of intelligent Willpower.

Regimes

Exercise No. 1. How many sounds are now demanding your attention? Count them. Listen! Try to distinguish: Their different *directions*; their different *causes*; their different *tones*; their difference in *strength*; their different *qualities*; their different *groupings*.

Repeat this exercise for ten days, with rest of two days, and on the tenth day, estimate the improvement made.

Exercise No. 2. Single out some one prominent sound, and note everything which you can possibly say about it.

Repeat this exercise ten times on the first day with a different sound. Repeat these exercises every day for ten days, with rest of two days, and on the tenth day, note the improvement.

Exercise No. 3. Select the faintest sound that continues coming to you. In doing this, try to distinguish some regular sound which you have not hitherto noticed. Note everything that can be said concerning it.

Repeat this exercise ten times on the first day, with a different sound. Repeat these exercises every day for ten days, with rest, and on the tenth day, note the improvement.

Exercise No. 4. Single out some one of the sounds that come regularly to you. Attend to this sound alone. Shut out all other sounds. Be filled with it. Become absorbed in it. Note everything which can be said of it.

Repeat this exercise ten times on the first day, with a different sound. Repeat these exercises every day for ten days, with rest, and on the tenth day note the improvement.

Exercise No. 5. Select the most pleasant sound that continues to come to you. Note all possible reasons for its pleasantness. Do not fall into reverie.

Repeat this exercise ten times on the first day with a different sound. Repeat these exercises every day for ten days, with rest, and on the tenth day, note the improvement.

Exercise No. 6. Listen carefully once to some simple melody played upon an organ or a piano. Try now to build up in your soul that melody entirely from memory. You may remember a note or two, but will forget the most of it. If, however, you are persistent, you can gradually reconstruct the lost tune. The author has often accomplished this building up of music. Make the exercise a frequent task.

Exercise No. 7. While one is striking the keys of a piano, first one, then another, endeavor, without looking at the player, to distinguish the notes, whether sharp or flat, position on the board, and the name of each note.

Repeat with two keys, one hand striking.

Repeat with four keys, both hands striking.

Repeat with full chord, one hand striking.

Repeat with full chords, both hands striking.

Practise in the above exercises should be continued until you can detect improvement in compass of hearing, correctness of hearing, control over hearing. Do not become discouraged. The purpose is Will. Resolve to go on to the end. That end is *Willpower.*

Do nothing without thought. Put the soul into the ear in all these exercises, willing, with great energy, attention to all sounds, or to one, or to none, as the case may be.

Carry the Mood of Will through every exercise.

Exclusion of sound is often an exhibition of Will, both in

the act of shutting sounds out, and in controlling the nerves in regard to sounds which refuse to vanish. Why, then, should not a more regulated and conscious mastery of ear be acquired?

Perhaps your hearing is defective and you are not aware of that fact. Or the defect may be due to a want of acute attention. In order to ascertain the real difficulty, the following exercise is suggested:

Exercise No. 8. When all is quiet, hold a watch at arm's length from the right ear. Do you hear it ticking? No? Move the watch gradually nearer the ear until you hear. Note the distance at which the ticking first becomes audible. Write the result and mark, "Ear No. 8", and the date. Repeat this exercise ten times on its first day. Repeat these exercises every day for ten days, with rest, and on the tenth day note, the improvement.

Meanwhile, induce several other persons to practise the same exercise so far as to ascertain the distance at which they can hear the ticking of the same watch.

During the ten days, repeat all the exercises with the left ear, correctly marking results.

If you make no improvement in hearing, this may still be due to a constitutional limit. Continue the practise until you are satisfied that your hearing cannot be improved. Then consult a physician.

If you do not hear as well as others, this also may be due to constitutional limit. It will, nevertheless, be wise to consult a physician.

Perhaps certain sounds which you hear incessantly are destroying you with the threat of nervous prostration or insanity. Your dear neighbor's piano played through everlasting hours, or his dog barking all night long, or street hawkers, become evidences of civilization's chaos. Procure the cessation of these sounds, if possible. If not, resolve to shut them out of the mind. Hence:

Exercise No. 9. Never fight disagreeable noises by attending to them. Select some particularly hateful sound which comes to you regularly. Make this a practice for the day. Now, by an enormous effort of Will attend so powerfully to some other sound or many sounds as to shut out the one you wish to banish. Continue this effort for five minutes. Do not become discouraged. You can do this act of exclusion if you will do it. After five minutes, rest, by turning the attention away from sounds in general. Then repeat the exercise by shutting out the sound for ten minutes. Give the matter a half-hour, increasing the time of exclusion of sound with each exercise a few minutes, and resting between efforts by diverting attention to other things.

Vary the effort to exclude sound by attending with great energy to some agreeable thought.

Do not will directly to shut a sound out of the ear. Will to become directly absorbed in other sounds or in other matters of thought. Repeat these exercises until you are a master at it.

Exercise No. 10. At night, when you are disturbed by hideous noises, stop thinking about them.

Insist that you do not care, anyway.

Think of a particularly pleasant tune; or thought; or experience. Do not work: take the matter easily.

Call up, mentally, a sound which is totally different from the one that disturbs you. Cause it to run in the mind, taking care that it has a certain regularity and rhythm. Imagine the loud ticking of a large clock, or the droning of an old-fashioned water-wheel, or the steady booming of the sea.

Remember, that all thought about the hateful sound only intensifies its power over you. To rage at a barking dog signifies one of two consequences: the death of the dog (possibly of its owner), or more nervousness on the part of the man who has no Will. Similarly, with other disturbing noises. The Will that masters them is a growing Will. The growing Will comes of intelligent exercise, with the Will-idea always present, "I

RESOLVE TO WILL! ATTENTION!"

Everybody knows how acute the hearing of the blind becomes, probably as Dr M.P. Hatfield has observed, "not because they have any better hearing than the rest of us, but because their misfortune makes them continually cultivate their hearing, for like all of our faculties, it is susceptible of very great improvement under cultivation".

CHAPTER X

EXERCISES IN TASTE

The German Physiologist, Valentin, could detect bitter at 100,000th of a solution of quinine.

> *Taste can be educated, as the nice discriminations of the professional tea-tasters show. In subconscious conditions, it is also abnormally acute.*
>
> —Text Book

Theory of This Chapter

A discriminating mind in taste;
A cultivated mind in taste;
Willed attention habituating the Mood of Will.

Preliminary

"The ordinary individual," remarks Mary Whiton Calkins in "An Introduction to Psychology", "asked to name what he had tasted at dinner, might respond with some such list as the following: beef-bouillon, roast duck, potato, onion, dressed celery, peach ice and coffee. But the psychologist would conclude at once that some of the tastes enumerated were complex experiences, made up of simpler elements. He would take means to isolate, so far as he could, the conditions of tastes, so that other sense-elements should be shut out from consciousness. He would select, as subject of the experiments, a person without smell-sensations, or else he would close the subject's nostrils, so as to eliminate most of these smell-sensations; and he would certainly blindfold the subject, to prevent his seeing the articles which he tasted. These substances would be presented to him at an even temperature, and the solids would be finely minced so as to be indistinguishable in form. Judging by the results of actual experiments, the results of such a test as applied to our suggested *menu,* would be the following: the blindfolded and anosmic (without smell-sensations) subject would as likely as not suppose that he had tasted chicken broth, beef, potato, an unknown sweetish substance, another unknown material mixed with a thick tasteless oil, a sweet unflavored substance and a slightly bitter liquid—perhaps a dilute solution of quinine. A normal person, also blindfolded, but without closed nostrils, would recognize the onion, the peach, the coffee and often the olive oil; but would be as likely to confuse the beef and the duck; whereas, if these were unsalted, the anosmic subject would fail to recognize them even as meats.

"What we know of the different tastes are complex experiences, made up of odors, motor experiences, pressure and pain sensations, visual elements and a far more limited number of taste-elements than we ordinarily suppose. The odor is the significant element in such 'tastes' as egg, milk, fruit, wine, onion, chocolate, coffee and tea. Tea and coffee are, indeed, undistinguished from quinine, when the odor elements are excluded, and are differentiated from each other only by the slight astringency of the tea, that is by the peculiar pressure-experience, the 'puckering', which it excites.

"The number of tastes seems to be four: sweet, salt, sour and bitter. But of the physical stimuli of taste-sensations, we know even less than of the indefinitely localized physiological organ. Chemically distinct substances may even arouse the same sensational quality, for example, both sugar and acetate of lead give a 'sweet' taste. Only one general statement may be hazarded: the taste-stimulus is always in liquid form. If the tip of the tongue be carefully dried, a crystal of sugar placed upon it will seem tasteless, until the tongue again becomes moist enough to dissolve it."

The experiments and investigations which have given us the meager knowledge we have on the subject of taste-sensations and their brain-area (little known), have all involved attention, discrimination, judgment, and so on. The object of the exercises in the present chapter has exactly similar ends in view—but above all, such work under direction as may make you better acquainted with yourself and give to you a greater scope of consciousness and self-control.

The tongue tastes; it also feels.

The sensation of touch is often confounded with that of taste. During a heavy cold in one's head, the tongue feels much, but tastes little. Aerated water gives the tongue a lively sensation of touch or feeling. Alum "draws" it. Pepper irritates it to burning. Some strong sweets are slippery. Some strong bitters are smooth. Cold food is lacking in the taste of warmer ones. The sensation produced by very cold water is largely that of feeling. Luke-warm coffee is not enjoyable because the aroma of its steam and the cold of ice are absent. The facts suggest some experiments.

Remember that the greatest mind is one which has, through the five senses, grasped the most of the outside world.

Regimes

Exercise No. 1. Procure a piece of alum. Merely touch it with the tongue. Now try to perceive its taste in distinction from its feeling. Repeat this exercise with other "puckery" substances. Repeat these experiments every day for ten days, with rest of two days, and on the tenth day, observe the improvement.

Exercise No. 2. Close the nostrils between the thumb and forefinger, and, touching the tongue with some "puckery" substance, try to perceive the taste. Is the idea of taste real or imaginary? Repeat with various similar articles. Repeat these exercises every day for ten days, with rest of two days, and on the tenth day, note the improvement.

Exercise No. 3. Place a little pepper on the tongue. Try to distinguish the taste from the irritation. Is there any difference? Repeat with other substances which "burn" the tongue. Repeat these exercises every day for ten days, with rest of two days, and on the tenth day, note the improvement.

Exercise No. 4. With white sugar or syrup placed on the tongue, try to distinguish whether the slippery feeling or the sweet taste is first perceived. Repeat these exercises every day for ten days, with rest, and on the tenth day, note the improvement.

Exercise No. 5. Sweeten equally two glasses of water. Let a friend, while you are not observing, place in one glass a minute quantity of quinine or other bitter substance. Now, taste and note which glass contains the drug by observing the greater sweetness of the water in which it has been placed. The quantity of "bitter" may be increased until additional sweetness can be perceived. If the water begins to taste bitter before increased sweetness is perceived, the experiment has failed. But do not be discouraged. Repeat until success is reached. Repeat these exercises every day for ten days, with rest, and on the tenth day, note the improvement.

Exercise No. 6. Try to recall, with great vividness—with the vividness of reality—from memory, the taste of various articles—sugar, lemon, quinine, onion, cheese, etc. Note whether one taste is recalled more vividly than another. Is such recalled taste always associated with a mental picture of its object, or is it abstract? Does the memory seem to be located in the brain or on the tongue? Whether in the brain or on the tongue, is it associated with some past experience? Now think of the tongue, and try to place the remembered sensation, abstracted from all past experience, there alone. That is difficult, but it can be done. Repeat these exercises every day for ten days, with rest, and on the tenth day, note the improvement.

Exercise No. 7. Procure six articles that are fragrant and six that have a pleasant taste. Arrange in pairs—one article of smell with one of taste, and so on until all are thus paired. Take one pair, and compare the sensation of smell with that of taste. Note similarity and difference between the sensations. Repeat with each pair. Repeat these experiments with articles that are odoriferous but not fragrant, and articles that have not an agreeable taste. Now note whether, in all tests with pairs of articles, the effect upon the "mind" is greater when the sensation is that of smelling than when it is that of tasting. Then note whether the difference or similarity of sensation is greater in the case of the first six articles (fragrant and pleasant) or in the case of the second six articles (odoriferous and unpleasant). What is the reason for the facts? Repeat these exercises every day for ten days, with rest, and on the tenth day, note the improvement.

Why is a meal of the same kind which is eaten in solitude with the same degree of hunger vastly less agreeable in itself than when eaten among pleasant companions? If this is not true, you evidently need lessons in sociability. With most people it is true. Eye, nose, tongue have changed not. Yet the meal looks better, smells better, tastes better. Is this due to imagination? Is there not, rather, a mutuality of ministration among the senses which requires the inspiration of friends to bring it fully out? A good eye, a good nose and a good tongue make a trinity of dining felicity. Add, then, a good heart and a pleasantly active soul, and the function of Willpower in the realm of vision, hearing and taste is discovered.

Exercise No. 8. While dining with friends, make the exercises of this chapter the subject of conversation and experiment so far as consistent with the business in hand, namely, dining in the most agreeable manner.

Exercise No. 9. It is a human privilege to put the soul into bodily sensations, or to withdraw it therefrom. In the one case, the word is *attention,* in the other case, it is *abstraction.* The following exercise deals with abstraction.

Secure the sensation of any taste or any smell. Now, resolutely try to recall from memory some other different sensation so vividly as to banish the first from the mind. For example: the smell of a rose, and then think strongly of the odor of onions. You must entirely forget the flower while thinking of the vegetable. Or, taste a little sugar, and then put the sensation out of the mind by recalling the memory of wormwood. Or the senses may, as it were, be crossed. Smell of a pink and banish the sensation by strong thought of the taste of pepper. Or taste alum and think about the smell of ammonia so keenly as to banish the first sensation. Repeat these exercises every day for ten days, with rest, and on the tenth day, note the improvement made.

After all, *abstraction* is only another name for *attention*—withdrawn from one quarter by being massed upon another. Whoever *attends* intelligently and masterfully to eye, nose, tongue, has either new worlds of pleasure or new guards against displeasure. Above all, has this person Will. Attention cultivated involves Will always present.

CHAPTER XI

EXERCISES IN SMELL

It is stated in Mr Stewart's account of James Mitchell, who was deaf, sightless and speechless, and, of course, strongly induced by his unfortunate situation to make much use of the sense we are considering, that his smell would immediately and invariably inform him of the presence of a stranger, and direct to the place where he might be; and it is repeatedly asserted that this sense had become in him extremely acute.—'It is related,' says Dr Abercrombie, 'of the late Dr Moyse, the well-known blind philosopher, that he could distinguish a black dress on his friends by its smell.'

—Professor Thomas C. Upham

Theory of This Chapter

Keenness of attention through discrimination in the sense of smell;
Persistently willed attention a feeder of Will;
A neglected sense cultivated and fullness and power of mind increased.

"In all ages of the world," Dr William Matthews has said, "a liberal allowance of proboscis has been admired, while a niggardly one has been held in contempt. The Romans liked a large nose, like Julius Caesar's; and it is a significant fact that the same word in Latin, *Nasutus,* means *having a large nose,* and *acute* or *sagacious.* All their distinguished men had snuff-taking organs not to be sneezed at. "In modern days, large noses have been not less coveted and esteemed than in the ancient. 'Give me,' said Napoleon, 'a man with a large allowance of nose. In my observations of men, I have almost invariably found a long nose and a long head go together.' "

Preliminary

"The faculty of scent may be cultivated like all other faculties, as is proven by blood-hounds and breeds of dogs which have been specially trained in this direction until it becomes an hereditary faculty. Those who deal in teas, coffees, perfumes, wine and butter, often cultivate their powers to a wonderful degree in their especial lines, but with the majority of people, it is the least cultivated of the senses, although Dr O.W. Holmes thinks it the one which most powerfully appeals to memory."

The sense of smell, it would seem, then, has been greatly neglected, as is seen in the fact that the names of odors are almost entirely artificial or derived from association. That it may be trained may be proved by any druggist or manufacturer of perfumes. The druggist does not recognize the "smell" of his own shop, but he perceives by the nose when he enters that of another. Always must he discriminate among odors in his business. The perfumist lives on the acuteness of his olfactory nerves. The glue-maker and soap-refiner exist in spite of their pursuits.

"We have little scientific knowledge of odors," says Calkins. "Even our names for them are borrowed, usually from the objects to which we chance to refer them, and occasionally even from their affective accompaniments. Thus, we know some odors only vaguely as good or bad, that is, pleasant or unpleasant, and at the best, we can say nothing more definite than 'heliotrope fragrance' or 'kerosene odor'. This chaotic state of affairs is largely due to the limited significance of odors in our intellectual and our artistic life.

"Many smells are, of course, like tastes, obviously complex experiences containing elements of taste, touch and vision, as well as of smell. The pungency of such smells as that of ammonia is thus a touch quality; and such experiences as smelling sour milk are perhaps due to the entrance of particles through the nose into the throat.

"The most satisfactory classification of smells, as we meet them in nature, is that adapted by the Dutch physiologist, Zwaardemaker, from the classification of Linnaeus. It recognizes the following classes:

"Ethereal smells, including all fruit odors.

"Aromatic smells, for example, those of camphor, spices, lemon, rose.

"Fragrant smells, for example, those of flowers.

"Ambrosiac smells, for example, all musk odors.

"Alliaceous smells, for example, those of garlic, asafoetida, fish.

"Empyreumatic smells, for example, those of tobacco and toast.

"Hircine smells, for example, those of cheese and rancid fat.

"Virulent smells, for example, that of opium.

"Nauseating smells, for example, that of decaying animal matter.

"We have sensational experiences, known as smells or odors, distinguished from each other, but not designated by special names; they are probably analyzable into a few distinct elements, but this analysis has never been satisfactorily made; and they are often compounded, and sometimes confused with tastes and touches.

"The structure of the physiological end-organs of smell is not very clearly made out. Two phenomena indicate, however, that these organs are so distinct that they correspond both with different physical stimuli and with different smell-experiences. One of these phenomena is that of exhaustion. Experimental investigations show, for example, that a subject 'whose organ is fatigued by the continuous smelling of tincture of iodine can sense ethereal oils almost or quite as well as ever, oils of lemon, turpentine and cloves but faintly, and common alcohol not at all.' Evidently, therefore, different parts of the end-organs are affected by these distinct smell-stimuli, else the nostrils would be exhausted for all smells at the same time.

"We know little of the physical conditions of smell. Two statements only can be made with any degree of assurance. It is highly probable, in the first place, that the smell-stimulus is always gaseous, not liquid; and it is almost certain that the property of stimulating the end-organs of smell is a function of the physical molecule, not of the atom, since most of the chemical elements are odorless. Summing up both physiological and physical conditions, we may say, therefore, that certain gaseous particles are carried by inspiration into the nostrils, where they stimulate cells found in the mucous membrane, and that these nerve-impulses are conveyed by the olfactory nerves to the temporal lobes of the brain."

The action of the olfactory nerves may be controlled by thought—that is by power of Will. Arranging paper tubes in such a way as to convey separate perfumes to each nostril, as suggested by Professor Scripture, "we can smell either one in preference to the other by simply thinking about it". An experiment may be made of this fact.

Regimes

Exercise No. 1. Take some fragrant flower. Inhale its odor. Walk about the room, away from the flower. Now, try to recall the quality and intensity of the smell. Repeat this exercise with various extracts and perfumes taken separately. Care must be had to give the nostrils sufficient rest between whiles, otherwise the sense of smell will become confused.

Repeat these exercises every day for at least ten days, with rest of two days. It will be better to go on until improvement is certainly noted in keenness of scent and mental power to describe smells or odors. On the tenth day, note the improvement.

During all the above and following practice, the feeling of strong Will must be kept constantly at the fore. *Put your soul into your nose.*

Exercise No. 2. Procure two different kinds of extracts. Inhale the odor of one. Do the same with the other. Think strongly of the first odor; then of the second. Now, try to compare them, noting the difference. Repeat this exercise every day for ten days, and on the tenth day, note the improvement.

Exercise No. 3. While sitting erect, gently inhale the air, and try to name any odor perceived. Is it real? Where does it originate? Let friends secrete some odoriferous substance in a room—a number of pinks or an open bottle of perfumery, not known to you, and while you are in another room. Enter and endeavor by smell alone to find the article. All other pronounced odors must be excluded from the place. Repeat these exercises every day for ten days, and on the tenth day, note the improvement.

Exercise No. 4. Ask some friend to hold in the hand an object which is not known to you and is fragrant or odoriferous. He is to hold the article at some distance from you, and then gradually to move it, held unseen in his two hands placed together, nearer and nearer, until you perceive the odor. Note the distance at which you perceive the object by smell. Can you name the smell? Can you name the object? Repeat the experiment with intervals of rest, with various different "smellable" articles.

Do you perceive some at a less distance than others? Why is this? Is it due to strength of odor or the quality? Repeat the exercise every day for ten days with rest of two days, and on the tenth day, note the improvement.

Humboldt declared that Peruvian Indians can, in the darkest night, determine whether a stranger, while yet far distant, is an Indian, European or Negro. The Arabs of the Sahara can detect by smell the presence of a fire forty miles away.

Exercise No. 5. Each of the five senses has the power of continually making new discoveries in the world of reality. Impressions appropriate to each may be related to the huge things of life. High living puts great significance into even the sense of smell. The present exercise may be made perpetual. Build up in your life the habit of associating the agreeable odors perceived in garden, field or wood, with true and great thoughts. Examples: new-mown hay—Whittier's poem, "Maud Muller"; sea-flats—Sidney Lanier's "Marshes of Glynn"; fresh-turned soil—the teeming life of the world; flowers—beauty regnant[5] in the earth. Such a habit will open new worlds, and it will develop energetic attention, and so tend to build up a strong Will in your life.

This work may be so conducted as to make improvement possible. Its value always depends upon the amount of soul put into it—that is, into the nose. The exercises will cultivate a neglected sense, but more, will develop a power of attention that will surprise you, and through this a power of Will, which is the end sought. The idea of Will must always be present. In every act, preserve the willing attitude.

---

[5]'Regnant' meaning reigning, ruling, predominant and widespread.

CHAPTER XII

EXERCISES IN TOUCH

The sense of touch is the most positive of all the senses in the character of its sensations. In many respects, it is worthy to be called the leading sense.

—Noah Porter

All the senses are modifications of the sense of touch.

—Demosthenes

Theory of this Chapter

Mind thrown into or abstracted from physical feeling at Will;
Will-attention making Will-action deliberative and second-nature;
Will prohibitions rendering mind supreme at least cost.

Preliminary

"The sensations of contact and temperature," says Royce, "are due to the excitation of points on the skin which differ for the various special sorts of experiences in question. Experiment shows that certain points of the skin are especially sensitive to stimulations given by cold objects, while other points are sensitive to disturbances due to hot objects. Our ordinary sensory experience of warmth or of cold is due to a complex excitement of many points of both these types. Still other points on the skin very wealthily interspersed among the others, give us, if excited in isolation, sensations of contact or of pressure.

Complex sensory excitations, due to the disturbances of the skin, sometimes with and sometimes without, notable accompanying organic disturbances, give us our experiences of hard and soft, of rough and smooth, of dry and moist objects."

There are many very curious facts to be observed in connection with touch. The degree of feeling arising from touch is usually dependent to a great extent upon attention. We do not, for example, ordinarily feel our clothing, but when thought turns to the matter, it becomes very apparent. If garments do not fit well, the nerves are likely to take on some habit of twitching or other unnatural movement. Such habits in children are often due to this fact. For the same reason, tickling sensations plague sleep away at night. That wise fool who calls himself a "business man" bolts his dinner in eight minutes, and tastes and feels nothing until dyspepsia makes taste and feeling perennial dominators of an unhappy existence. Another fool consumes alcohol in winter for warmth and in summer for coolness; the secret of its "beneficent" ministry is its paralyzing power over physical consciousness. In latter days, this man feels heat and cold with the keenness of a skeleton veiled in the rotten gauze of ruined nerves. The orator who is absorbed in his flights regards not the busy fly upon his nose nor the physical pain which was insistent before his soul afire took mastery of sense. The epicure, every sense to the fore, lingers while he dines, and nourishes delighted boon fellowship with kindred spirits. When the orator has it before him to listen to another man's lucubrations[6], his fly becomes a Dante for torture, and his pains possess the power of a Spanish Inquisition. So, too, when Xantippe[7] appears at the philosophers' board, the world must lose in Socratic wisdom.

To attend or not to attend is always with feeling an important question. The end nerves may be brought under large control

---

[6]Lucubration: laborious work, study, thought, etc., esp. done at night.

[7]Xantippe: wife of Socrates, late 5th century B.C.

of the Will. The soldier frequently fails to note that his arm has been shot off in the onslaught of a charge. Your tooth will cease aching if your house is afire or your horse is running away with you. If feeling may be thus dissipated, it may, as well, be called in and controlled by the exercise of Will. Exercises in touch are, therefore, suggested for development of Will.

Regimes

Exercise No. 1. Pass the ends of each finger of the right hand in turn very lightly over any flat uncovered surface. Try first a surface which is rough; then one which is smooth. Note the difference in "feel" between a rough surface and a smooth. This will require a good deal of attention, for the difference is manifold. Repeat these exercises with several rough and smooth surfaces. Repeat as above with the fingers of the left hand. Note whether the feeling is greater with one hand than with the other. Now repeat the experiments with cloth—of linen, cotton, woolen, silk. The "feel" of each material is peculiar. Compare, by act, the sense of touch as given by one piece of cloth with that given by another. Continue these exercises with several pieces of cloth in pairs. Repeat with one hand, then with the other. What is the main "feel" of silk? Of cotton? Of woolen? Of linen? Have you any sensation other than touch with any of these kinds of cloth? If so, is it disagreeable? Then resolve to handle that variety of cloth until the aversion has been mastered. This can be done, as clerks in great department stores will testify. Repeat all the exercises here given every day for ten days, and on the tenth day, note the improvement in touch—delicacy, kinds of sensations produced, etc.

Exercise No. 2. Practise touching lightly the surface of an uncovered table, with the separate fingers, one after the other, of each hand. Note the degree of steadiness with which this is done. Now repeat the experiment with strong pressure upon each finger of the hands separately applied. What is the difference in sensation between the light touch and the strong pressure? Repeat the exercise every day for ten days, with rest, and on the tenth day, note the improvement in discrimination.

Exercise No. 3. Grasp a small object, say, a paperweight or a rubber ball, very lightly, for just an instant, dropping it immediately. Then grasp it firmly, and instantly drop it. Did you feel the object with each finger in the first instance? In the second? Make no mistake. What, if any, difference in sensation did you observe? This requires that the Will command great attention. Hence, it cannot be done carelessly. Repeat every day for ten days, with rest, and on the tenth day, note the improvement in touch and power of discrimination and attention.

Exercise No. 4. Look at the back of either hand. Now twist the second finger toward you and cross the first finger behind it. While the fingers are so crossed, press the unsharpened end of a lead-pencil between the finger ends. Look sharp! Do you seem to feel one pencil or two? Shut the eyes and repeat the experiment. Again, is the sensation of one pencil or two? Is the deception stronger with eyes closed or open?

When is the pressure of the pencil between the crossed fingers light? Or when is it strong? Explain the fact that there are apparently two pencils. Repeat the experiment with three pairs of fingers. Repeat every day for ten days, with rest, and on the tenth day, note the improvements in the various respects suggested.

The eyes being closed in the first experiment, you will probably thrust the pencil against the side of the third finger, which is now on the outside of the hand. Explain this little mistake.

Exercise No. 5. With eyes closed, place several objects, promiscuously and separated, upon a table. The eyes still being closed, move the right hand lightly over the objects and endeavor to estimate the several distances which separate them. Do not measure by length of hand or finger. Repeat the exercise with the left hand. Keep the question in mind: which hand is more nearly correct in judgment. Repeat every day for ten days, with rest, and on the tenth day, note the improvement.

Exercise No. 6. While your eyes are closed, ask a friend to present to you, so that you can examine by touch alone, but not by taking in your hand, several small objects, one after another. Now try to determine what the articles are. Examples: small onion, small potato, flower bulb, piece of dry putty, piece of amber, piece of wax; or some sugar, sand, ground pepper, salt, etc. Repeat every day for ten days, with rest, and on the tenth day, note the improvement.

Exercise No. 7. Procure small blocks of any material—wood, iron—round in shape, and of exactly the same size, but differing slightly in weight. Say two blocks weigh each 1 ounce, two 1 ½ ounces each, two 2 ounces each, and so on to a dozen, always having two blocks of the same weight. Let the weights be stamped or written on one side of the blocks only.

Place them promiscuously on a table, blank side up. Close the eyes and at random pick up one block and then a second, using the same hand. Determine by "feel" whether the weights so picked up are equal or not. Estimate the weights in each experiment. Repeat with the left hand. Repeat with both hands, used alternately. Repeat the experiment in all cases many times. Continue every day for ten days, with rest, and on the tenth day, note the improvement in judgment.

Exercise No. 8. Procure twenty-four small wooden models of crystals, cut from blocks about three inches square. Throw them promiscuously all at once upon a table. With eyes closed, take one in the hand and observe the mental picture that arises by the sense of touch. Count the faces, lines, angles. Now open the eyes and note the difference between this mental picture and the reality. This experiment will be difficult because you are not familiar with the forms of crystals, and judgment is left to touch alone. To assist, therefore, look at the crystal models until you are able to shut the eyes and perceive with the eye of the mind the form just examined. Repeat every day for ten days, with rest, and on the tenth day, note the improvement in judgment.

Exercise No. 9. When you shake hands with people, note in their grasp any index of their character that may be suggested. Cultivate the gently-firm grasp. Instantly rebuke the bone-crusher; he has a vice which needs destruction. Is the touch of some hands disagreeable to you? Note in what particular irks you. Be not ruled by that aversion, but seek such hands, and resolve to throw off the feeling. This may be useful to you in the "control of others". The effort to overcome an aversion always develops Will. Determine that nothing which you must touch more or less habitually shall control the sensation which it produces. Let this aversion be a type of all tyrannous aversions. Such an aversion means the inability of a small mind to divert its attention. The really large soul masters such irritations and dislikes. But the guide and controller here is Will. Every aversion conquered signifies power of Will increased.

"ATTENTION! I RESOLVE TO WILL!"

CHAPTER XIII

EXERCISES FOR THE NERVES

Standing at the center of the universe, a thousand forces come rushing in to report themselves to the sensitive soul-center. There is a nerve in man that runs out to every room and realm in the universe.

Man's mechanism stands at the center of the universe with telegraph-lines extending in every direction. It is a marvelous pilgrimage he is making through life while myriad influences stream in upon him.

Some Faraday shows us that each drop of water is a sheath for electric forces sufficient to charge 800,000 Leyden jars, or drive an engine from Liverpool to London. Some Sir William Thomson tells us how hydrogen gas will *chew up a large iron spike as a child's molars* will *chew off the end of a stick of candy.*

—Newell Dwight Hillis

Theory of this Chapter

Cessation of unnecessary motion conserves force;
Control of nerves tones up body and mind, and increases the sum total of personal power;
Habituated control of nervous energy exercises and therefore strengthens and regulates the Will.

Preliminary

Sir Michael Foster once said: "When physiology is dealing with those parts of the body which we call muscular, vascular, glandular tissues, and the like, rightly handled, she points out the way, not only to mend that which is hurt, to repair the damages of bad usage and disease, but so to train the growing tissues and to guide the grown ones as that the best use may be made of them for the purposes of life. She not only heals; she governs and educates. Nor does she do otherwise when she comes to deal with the nervous tissues. Nay, it is the very prerogative of these nervous tissues that their life is, above that of all the other tissues, contingent on the environment and susceptibility to education."

We are conscious of sensations apprehended through the various sense organs. But we are possessed of what is called "general consciousness". One may discover this by sitting for a little time in a room that is perfectly still. The general testimony of the nervous system will then be perceived. The movement of the heart may be felt; the breathing may become audible; a murmur may perhaps be noticed in the ears; a general feeling of warmth or coolness will be observable. You are alive! You are aware of yourself in a physical sense. You are conscious in particular spots, to be sure, but in a general way also over almost the entire body. With this "general consciousness", we begin the exercises of the present chapter. They are important. Do not slight them.

Regimes

Exercise No. 1. Attend to this "general consciousness" a few moments. Sit quietly, exclude from the mind all external matters, and take cognizance of the whole body. Put your entire thought upon this one thing; it will be difficult, for you will desire to think of a thousand foreign things; but it can be done by persistence and patient willing. Now write out every fact that makes itself known to you by the testimony of the body. Repeat every day for ten days, with rest of two days. On the tenth day, compare the records. Observe the sum total of facts made known. Note also any improvement in power of attending to "general consciousness" and reports of facts or sensations.

Exercise No. 2. Sitting quietly in a room which is undisturbed, attend as before a few moments to "general consciousness". Now throw consciousness to some particular part of the body. Let it be the arm from hand to elbow. Put the whole mind there. Exclude all sensations except those that arise there. What are the reports? Write these facts for reference.

Repeat this exercise with the hand. With the shoulder. With the back. With the foot. And so on, with different parts of the body. Always get at the facts testified by consciousness.

Repeat this exercise with the head. Now attend wholly to hearing—not to sounds, but to the sensation of hearing—in the ears. Again, give undivided attention to sight: let the whole mind be at the eyes, not on the objects of vision.

Now press upon some spot in the body, say, the back of a hand, or on one cheek, and, while doing so, locate attention at some other spot so resolutely as to forget the sensation of pressure. Write the results in each case. Repeat every day for ten days with rest. On the tenth day, compare the records and note the sum total of facts reported, together with any improvement in the number of facts observed and the power of attention gained.

Exercise No. 3. Walk about the room slowly and quietly, keeping the mind wholly upon "general consciousness". Now rest a moment. Repeat—always retaining your hold on consciousness, never allowing it to wander—ten times. Make a record of the most prominent facts reported. Repeat every day for ten days, with rest. On the tenth day, compare the records and note results, as before.

Exercise No. 4. Stand erect in a quiet room, and pass through a regular series of exercises *without weights.*

- Move the right arm, slowly and evenly, directly up from the shoulder, six times. Keep your mind on the work.
- From the shoulder, directly out in front, six times.

- From the shoulder, directly out to the right, six times.
- With the right hand at arm's length above the shoulder, swing the whole arm in a semi-circle, arm straight, directly down in front, bringing hand to leg, without bending the body, six times.
- From the original position down to the right side of the leg, six times.
- With the right arm extended at the right side straight out from the shoulder, swing it around in front until the hand is directly before the face, six times.
- With the right hand and arm, reverse all the above movements.
- Repeat the same movements with the left hand, six times.
- With the left hand and arm, reverse all the movements.

Remember: these movements must be made deliberately and slowly. Attend to each exercise with the whole mind. Do not permit wandering thoughts. Put the entire thought of yourself into every act. Be wholly conscious of what you are doing. Above all, keep the sense of willing present during each movement. Thrust the Will out into the very muscles.

Repeat every day for ten days, with rest. Or indefinitely.

Exercise No. 5. Stand erect in a quiet room. Without supporting yourself with the hands, swing the right foot directly out in front as far as possible while retaining the balance of the body. Return it to the floor in former position. Make these movements deliberately and slowly, six times.

- Swing right foot out to right, sidewise. Return to former position, six times.
- Swing right foot out in front, around to right, back to position, six times.
- Swing right foot back and out and up as far as possible, preserving balance. Return to position, six times.
- Swing right foot back as before, around in a semi-circle

past right side, back to position, six times.

- Reverse each movement with right foot, six times.
- Repeat all movements with left foot, six times.
- Repeat these exercises every day for ten days, with rest.

The work here suggested must be performed with great vigor, yet slowly and deliberately, with intense thoughtfulness.

Exercise No. 6. Stand erect in a quiet room. Look straight ahead. Slowly turn the face far around to the right, and return, six times.

- Look ahead. Turn the face slowly to the left, and return, six times.
- Bend the head slowly back as far as possible, and return, six times.
- Bend the head slowly forward and down, as far as possible, and return, six times.
- Drop the head forward on the chest. Slowly swing it to the right, in a circle up to the right, to the left backward down and back to the left shoulder, to the right in a circle down to the former position, six times.
- Drop the head back between the shoulders. Swing it, to the right up in a circle to the right shoulder, to the left down around in front and up to the left shoulder, to the right down and back to former position, six times.
- Repeat all exercises every day for ten days, with rest.

Exercise No. 7. Stand erect in a quiet room. With the mind upon the act, slowly lift the right shoulder up as far as possible, and return in like manner to natural position, six times.

- Repeat with the left shoulder, six times. Repeat the exercises ten times for ten days, with rest.

Exercise *No. 8.* Stand erect in a quiet room. Without moving the feet, twist the body slowly around as far as possible, to the right, then to the left. Practise six times.

- Stand erect, hands hanging prone at the sides. Bend the

body at the hips; straightforward and down in front; to the right; to the left. Practice six times.

- Repeat the exercises every day for ten days, with rest, as above.

These exercises are designed to be suggestive. They can be varied. Nevertheless, an order should be determined upon and rigidly followed. Perform all acts slowly, deliberately, with the mind intently fixed upon the movement. Keep the Will-idea present. Throw this thought into the limbs and muscles: "I RESOLVE TO WILL! ATTENTION!"

Exercise No. 9. Stand erect. Concentrate thought upon self. Now let the mind affirm, quietly, resolutely, without wandering: "I am receiving helpful forces! I am open to all good influences! Streams of power for body and mind are flowing in! All is well!" Repeat these and similar assertions calmly yet forcibly many times. Do not be passive. Keep the sense of willing strongly at the fore. Will to be in the best possible moral condition. Rise to the mood of the three-fold health: of body, of mind, of soul.

- Continue this exercise for fifteen minutes, with brief intervals of rest, at least every morning of your life.
- Whenever worried or perplexed or weary, go into this assertive mood and welcome the forces of the good. These directions if followed will prove of priceless value to you.

Exercise No. 10. Stand erect. Summons a sense of resolution. Throw Will into the act of standing. Absorbed in self, think calmly but with power these words: "I am standing erect. All is well! I am conscious of nothing but good!" Attaining the Mood indicated, walk slowly and deliberately about the room. Do not strut. Be natural, yet encourage a sense of forcefulness. Rest in a chair. Repeat, with rests, fifteen minutes.

- Repeat every day indefinitely.

Exercise No. 11. Stand erect. In the same Mood of Will, advance slowly to a table and take a book in the hand, or move a chair, or go to the window and look out. Every act must be a willed act, and full of Will.

- Repeat every fifteen minutes with at least six different objects.
- Continue the exercises indefinitely.

Exercise No. 12. After a moment's rest, deliberately walk up to a chair and be seated. Force Will into the act. Do not lop down. Do not seat yourself awkwardly. Do not sit stiffly, but easily, yet erect. Now, with the whole mind on the act of getting up, slowly rise. Try to be graceful, try to be natural, for Will may add grace to nature. Cultivate the erect posture, whether sitting, standing or walking. Cultivate the vital sense in all movements. By the vital sense is meant the feeling, "I am alive! Splendidly alive!" If you are thin-blooded, dyspeptic and nervous, this may at first be difficult, but it will greatly help you.

- Repeat every fifteen minutes.
- Continue indefinitely.

Exercise No. 13. The nervous system is very apt to become a tyrant. When it is shattered, or overtaxed, adequate rest and a physician are imperative demands. But many people who regard themselves as well are subject to its tyranny. This may be due in part to a want of self-control. The following directions may appear to be absurd; nevertheless, they suggest a way out of some nervous difficulties:

Sometimes, when you are restive, you experience, on retiring, "creeping" sensations in the hair of your head; the back of your neck "tickles"; a needle is suddenly thrust into your arm, or a feather seems to be roaming here and there over your physiology. Distracted and robbed of sleep, one spot is slapped, another is pinched, another rubbed, while slumber merely "hangs around". How long is this torture to continue? So long as, and no longer than, you permit. Why should one be thus pestered? One needs not to be. It is simply a matter of Will and persistence. If you have practised the suggestions relating to attention and abstraction, you have already acquired power over your nerves by the dominance of mind. In regard to all such matters, therefore, cultivate the ability *to turn the mind elsewhere.* So long as one slaps and rubs and pinches, so long will sensations diabolic continue. Cultivate indifference to the fly by ignoring it. Do not think about it at all. Put the mind upon some important and absorbing subject of interest. Will that a particular "tickle" shall appear at some other place, making choice of the exact spot; it will obey, and meanwhile, you will forget it. If it does not, will it from one place to another, and finally with that it shall vanish; it will certainly obey in the end. Similarly with regard to any other distracting "feeling".

As a matter of fact, everyone exerts such self-control in a thousand instances daily. The clock's ticking is unnoticed; the railway train is not heard; the huckster's voice is not perceived; cattle low, and birds sing, and children shout, and a city roars, while the mind continues unmindful. Busy men who are surrounded by dense populations, and residents of Niagara, hear neither the "indistinguishable babble" of life nor the thunder of Nature. Shakespeare has said:

> "The crow doth sing as sweetly as the lark
> When neither is attended; and, I think,
> The nightingale, if she should sing by day,
> When every goose is cackling, would be thought
> No better a musician than the wren."

The accustomed ear is deaf to the world. But the Will hides behind the tympanum to make custom its beneficent muffler.

You should bear in mind that there is deep design in the back of these exercises and tests offered for your use. You are pursuing this study for the sole reason that you wish increased power of Will. And precisely this you will secure if you earnestly follow the instructions given.

"There is one consolation, too, in the carrying out of these tasks. Not a jot or tittle of the effort expended will be lost or wasted. All is deposited in a very safe bank. What Professor Sedgwick has said of mind-culture is equally true of will-culture: 'It is impossible to estimate the ultimate good to be derived in indirect ways from any bit of mental cultivation one manages to give oneself.' Not only is nothing lost, but a profit which bears an analogy to compound interest, is derived. The will is not only laying by a supply of willpower, but by its various exercises, it is increasing its own efficiency in winning willpower. The progression is geometrical. *It adds to itself its own newly acquired willpower, and thus strengthened, it gains more and more.*"

"ATTENTION! I RESOLVE TO WILL!"

CHAPTER XIV

EXERCISES FOR THE HANDS

I am, and have been, any time these thirty years, a man who works with his hands—a handicraftsman. If the most nimble-fingered watch-maker among you will come to my workshop, he may set me to put a watch together, and I will set him to dissect, say, a blackbeetle's nerves. I do not wish to vaunt, but I am inclined to think that I shall manage my job to his satisfaction sooner than he will do his piece of work to mine.

—Thos. H. Huxley

Theory of this Chapter

The hand, mind's executive organ; The consequent need of a perfect executor;
Culture of mind through mastery of hands;
Enormous reaction upon Willpower of culture of mind resolutely determined in manual training.

The hands are said to indicate, in a general way, the nature of their owner. The so-called "science of palmistry" is based on the inner lines of the hand, and the delicate curving lines of the finger-ends are now observed in prison studies for the identification of criminals. Yet few people know their own hands. This is because few people really understand the one condition of all knowledge, *attention.*

Nevertheless, the hand is one of the most perfect and obedient of servants. Industry, invention, science, art, reveal the range of its nobility, according to the soul behind it. To the ditch-digger, it may be a claw only; to the painter and sculptor an instrument of creative power. A catapult or a wound-dresser, a sword-wielder or a swayer of the pen, a food producer or a mind-revealer, a tool or an instrument of the noblest humanity, the hand is servant and king among the senses, an index of spirit-values, a prophet of all the future.

Preliminary

The hand is the executive organ of the body.

As the body is the instrument of mind, the hand, therefore, becomes mind's chief officer in life.

The savage wills to procure flesh for food: the outcome is the spear, the bow and arrow, the hook and net.

The hunter wills a permanent shelter: the outcome is the hammer, the axe, the saw, the trowel, nails and various building materials.

The house-dweller wills agriculture: the outcome is the spade, the pickaxe, the shovel, the hoe, the plow, the rake, the sickle, scythe, cradle, mower, reaper, thresher, mill.

The farmer wills education: the outcome is pen, ink and paper, the printing-press, the laboratory, the microscope and telescope, the library, the school and college.

The educated soul wills art: the outcome is the chisel and mallet, the brush and pallet, the canvas and the museum.

The artistic mind wills music: the outcome is the reed, string, horn—orchestral talent.

These all will government: the outcome is the throne and scepter, the constitution, the court and council-rooms, the sword, gun, treaty.

Man wills religion: the outcome is the altar, the Book, the Church, the Rubric, the Concrete Philanthropy of Soul.

Every single step in this long journey, the hand has been omnipresent as the Executive of the Conquering Will.

Training of the hand always reacts upon the growing mind. It may become a medium by which to culture the soul and develop the Will. Like Will—like hand. But as well, like hand—like Will. Whoever puts his whole hand to the growth of Willpower, has power of will wholly in hand.

Regimes

The following should be practised:

Exercise No. 1. Examine the hands carefully. Get acquainted with them. Note their peculiarities, so intently and thoughtfully that you can form a mental picture of them with closed eyes.

- Slowly move the limp fingers of the right hand toward the palm until they touch it, and return in the same manner, six times.
- Repeat while bringing the thumb in the same manner under to meet the fingers six times.
- Repeat with stiffened muscles, each exercise above, six times.
- With hand extended, open, slowly spread fingers and thumb from one another, and return to touch, six times.
- Repeat all exercises with the left hand, six
- Repeat every day for ten days, with rest of two days.

What is the value of these directions? None at all, unless you *think,* and above everything else, put Will into each movement.

Exercise No. 2. Saw off six inches of an old broom-handle. Stand erect. Fill the lungs. With the right hand held straight out in front and at arm's length, grasp the piece of wood, and slowly and gradually grip the same, beginning with light pressure and increasing to the limit of strength. Repeat six times.

- Repeat with the arm straight out at the right side, six times.
- Repeat with the arm straight up from the right shoulder, six times.

- Repeat with the arm prone at the right side, six times.
- Repeat with the arm straight back from the right side, and held up as far as possible, six times.
- Now exercise the left hand in the same manner, following the order above indicated. The exercises may be alternated between the right hand and the left. Example: Entire exercise with right hand; same with left, twelve times. Also, each part of exercise with right and left hands, twelve times.

Remember, the lungs should be inflated during each movement, and a slight rest should be indulged from time to time. Above all, a sense of Will must be kept strongly in mind. Repeat every day for ten days, with rest of two days.

Exercise No. 3. Procure a spring-balance weighing scale, registering ten or twelve pounds. Insert the broomhandle in ring. Drive a nail into a table, the length of the balance from the edge, and enough more to permit the thumb of the hand grasping the wood to curve under the table edge and cling. Now throw the balance-hook over the nail, grasp the wood with fingers of the right hand, thumb under table edge, and by finger movement only (do not pull with the arm) draw on the balance as hard as possible. The balance-hook must pull on nail far enough from the edge of the table to prevent the fingers while drawing as suggested from quite touching the palm of the hand.

- Repeat, with intervals of rest, six times.
- Make a dated record of pull indicated in pounds and fractions, mark right hand, and preserve.
- Repeat with the left hand, six times.
- Continue every day for ten days, with rest.

On the tenth day, compare the records and note progress.

In this work, never fail an instant to put Will into each movement.

In particular, note, from time to time, whether or not you can increase pulling power of fingers by sheer exercise of Will. Observe which hand registers greater improvement in given time.

Exercise No. 4. Rest for two days from the tenth day. Repeat the above exercises with right and left hands alternately, six times in all, while someone is playing upon any good instrument a strong and rapid musical composition. Make record as before.

- Continue for ten days, with rest. Summons constantly a feeling of the greatest resolution possible, during all movements.
- On the tenth day, compare records and note improvement in each hand. Observe which hand has now made the greatest improvement.
- Observe especially whether music has seemed to increase Willpower. Explain that fact.

Exercise No. 5. Imagine that you hold a revolver in the right hand. Now think of pulling the trigger. Throw a sense of great energy into the finger, but do not move it. Now hold the breath and repeat the imaginary act. Do you feel energy in the finger as before? Resolve to do so. Will mightily to that end.

- Repeat with all fingers in turn. Right hand. Left hand. Six times.
- Repeat for ten days. Observe the final improvement.

Exercise No. 6. Set the hands to the learning of some useful mechanical trade—the skillful use of various tools, as carving, engraving, cabinet-making. If already so employed, take up some musical instrument, or drawing, or painting. Resolve to master one thing! Persist until the goal is yours.

Exercise No. 7. Strive to cultivate and maintain a feeling of nice and confident skill while engaged in any manual work, as advised in "*Business Power*" under the caption, "Skilled Craftsmanship". "The idea is a sense in consciousness of *nicety, delicacy, perfection,* in every member of the body, used at any time. This gives harmony between the conscious and the deeper or subconscious self—a harmony always needful to the best work. One man is the 'bull in the China closet'; another is deftness itself. As a matter of fact, the most skillful persons possess this consciousness without being particularly aware of it."

Exercise No. 8. "The best results demand a man's best conscious powers on the matter in hand. You are urged to multiply yourself into what you do. But in doing a thing skillfully, having the skilled *feeling* developed, you really depend on the acquired habits and ability which previous thought has 'bedded down' in the deeper self. You should, therefore, remember that the trained deeper self may be trusted. Oftentimes, when your ordinary thinking becomes overanxious or 'flurried', you confuse your own skill. Some things which we do perfectly without conscious effort, we immediately 'muss up' if we try carefully to attend to all details. Do not permit the hurried feeling to take possession of your nerves. When such feeling does occur, quiet yourself by an act of Will; turn, if necessary, to other work for a time, and thus prevent the habit of unsteadiness of spirit and body, so obviating 'hair-trigger' conditions and a thousand blunders."

Exercise No. 9. Above all, never permit yourself to be pushed in your work beyond a pace consistent with the best results. Remember, when the mind is steady the hand is almost sure to follow that condition.

These exercises may be continued with profit, provided the idea of Will is everlastingly borne in mind.

CHAPTER XV

GENERAL HEALTH

Carrying any business or study in the mind all the time, day and night, morning and evening, does not really advance that business so much as forgetting it at intervals and letting the mind rest, as you allow your muscles to rest after any physical exertion. Mind allowed to rest gains new ideas and new force to carry out ideas. What is the remedy? More recreation. More variety of occupation. More selves in our one self. To attain the highest and happiest life we need to have two, and possibly three, if not four lives in one—to be merchant in the morning and artist or yachtsman or something else in the afternoon, and in the second life forget for the time all about the first, and in such forgetfulness rest the first life or set of faculties, recuperate them, refresh them, and go back to business, or art, or science, or any occupation, next day, with more force, plan, idea, thought to put in it.

—Prentice Mulford

Theory of this Chapter

State of Will depends upon condition of physical health;
Physical health is a goal of science, and is reached through the resolute and persistent Will;
Every rule of health deliberately followed becomes a developer of Willpower.
The momentum of a well person thrown into Will-culture is enormous, and is certain of great attainments.

A condition of general health is of paramount importance

to development of Will. In a sense, Willpower is emphatic personality, and the emphasis of personal resolution, which is the strong Will, depends largely upon physical conditions. There are great Wills in feeble bodies, but this is probably the exception. The influence of pain, discouragement, invalidism, upon our power of willing, is well known. Ordinarily, a man's average power of Will is determined by his average of health. "Hence vigorous self-determination depends upon plentiful and wholesome blood supply, or ultimately upon good food well digested and good air well inhaled. The secret of energy, and even of ethics, in the last analysis, is largely in sound digestion and good ventilation. Lessen or vitiate the supply of blood, and you may produce any desired degree of inaction and helplessness. On the contrary, cerebral congestion in a vigorous person (as in the insane) may generate tremendous outbursts of muscular activity and stern resolution."

Undoubtedly, the mind exercises a great influence over the body, and when sufficient Willpower can be mustered to banish fear and nervousness, and to summons a strong psychic condition, certain forms of ailing or disease may be benefited or even cured. "Will to be well! This, strictly speaking, is the 'mind cure'; is potent in nerve diseases, and is not useless in other maladies." Every intelligent physician understands this and seeks to cultivate in his patients the helpful, assertive and hopeful mood of mind. "A strong motive to live positively keeps some people alive," said a noted Scotch physician.

But the mind is influenced by the body. Frequently such influence masters the soul before Will can be summoned, and to such a degree that the necessary sense of Will can no more be put forth than a determination to perform a physical or religious miracle. Hence, the best advice of common sense in regard to health would attempt to combine these forces of nature—proper attention to physical conditions, a resolute state of Will, and tried and proved medical practice. But see Rule 14 below.

"Nevertheless, it is important fully to understand," as Dr A.T. Schofield remarks in "The Unconscious Mind", "that when the brain is restored to health by good nerve tissue and healthy blood, it can be made by suggestion to exercise as healthy an influence over the body as previously it exercised a harmful one. If ideal centers can produce ideal diseases, surely the rational cure is to bring these ideal centers into a healthy condition, and then make them the means of curing the ideal disease. Mental disease requires, and can ultimately only be cured by, mental medicine."

In time of peace, prepare for war. In time of health, fortify against disease. Here notice

Some Important Rules

Rule 1. Food should be regulated according to peculiarities of body and general work performed. Water which is pure should be freely drunk. Plenty of sound sleep should be secured, and slumber should be enhanced by plenty of pure air. Most people drink too little water. The air of many sleeping rooms would kill a person. Regularity of habits should be cultivated. Sufficient exercise must be taken to keep the muscles from degeneration and to vitalize the blood by activity of lungs.

Rule 2. Rest is also important. For the laboring man absolute idleness is not always rest; interested activity which brings unused muscles into play is better. This general truth lies at the bottom of popular employment of the day called Sunday. But such employment is largely injurious rather than beneficial. It frequently involves wrong methods as well as various excesses. The most wholesome rest as yet discovered for that day is suggested by religion. If you sneer at this proposition, that shows that you do not know what real religion is—or that your Will is set in directions contrary to the deepest instincts of mankind. There are people who are always too tired to attend religious exercises on

Sunday, who nevertheless waste health in other ways, or dawdle around with listless energies that exercise neither mind nor muscles. The normally and intelligently religious person never complains that his observance of the Day wearies or unfits him for the week following. To be sure, it is possible to "dissipate" in this matter, and some people shoulder the universe while church bells are ringing, leaving, apparently little for the Almighty to accomplish alone. Nevertheless, testimony agrees that a healthful religious use of Sunday tones the system in every department. This is not Puritanism; it is common sense. The laboring man would improve his condition if he would quit his enemies and ally himself with at least a little semblance of sound reason.

Rule 3. Above all, anger, irritation, jealousy, depression, sour feelings, morose thoughts, and worry, should be forever banished from the mind by the resolute, masterful Will. All these are physiological devils. They not only disturb the mind, but also injure the body by developing poisons and distorting cells. They prevent an even circulation. The poisons which they generate are deadly in the extreme. They induce more or less permanent physiological states which are inimical to vigorous Will. They dispel hopefulness, and obscure high motives, and lower the mental tone. They should be cast out of life with the resolution that as aliens they shall always be treated.

Regimes

Rule 4. Resolve, then, upon the following perpetual regimes:

1. Determine to live in a regular manner. Nevertheless, be master of rules, not slave.
2. Shun rich pastries and foods and drink which stimulate but do not nourish.
3. Keep the body clean. Bathe frequently, always rinsing in fresh water, cooler than the first, unless you are

convalescent, and dry thoroughly.

Rule 5. Attention! A bit of perfumery dropped into the bath, or applied thereafter, will cultivate physical pride—not vanity—which will prize the body and make clean flesh a delight.

Rule 6. After vigorous drying rub and knead and slap for a few minutes. If the bath has been taken during the day, keep up a gentle but resolute activity a short time before going out of the dressing-room. Then assume a self-possessed and assertive mood of mind, with Will strongly at the fore.

If the bath is taken before retiring, get into a clean garment, and then sprawl over every foot of bed-linen, of a proper temperature, luxuriating, resting, conscious of being a clean and very good sort of person. Now note with shut eyes what you see of colors and shapes in the inky darkness before you sleep.

Rule 7. Drink at least four full glasses of *pure* water every day unless you are too fleshy, in which case consult a physician. For most people, more would probably be better. In addition, drink whenever you want water, except when heated. If heated, refresh the mouth by rinsing, but do not swallow for a time. Of course it is here supposed that you have stopped exercise in a heated condition. Drink at your meals, before, after. Don't gulp ice-water. Don't boil your stomach with hissing hot water. A good drink is composed of rather hot water with milk to color well, and enough salt to taste. Drink water freely before retiring for the day.

Rule 8. Make sure of pure air in your sleeping room. Don't sleep in a draft. If possible sleep with head away from open door or window. Place a light screen between yourself and the source of air. See to it, however, that the pure air can get to you. Don't sleep in a hot room. Don't sleep in a freezing atmosphere.

Rule 9. Keep your sleeping room clean. Make it attractive. That room ought to be the best in the house. If it is a small hired room, sacrifice many things for furniture, pictures, ornaments, articles of toilet. Do not suppose that, because you are a male biped, you are above these suggestions. You are occupied with dirt all day; why not get away from dirt at night? Man is an animal with a soul, and therefore, may not wisely "bunk down" like a dog, or "stall in" like a horse or an ox.

Rule 10. Keep your body and clothing as clean as possible. Labor, in a clean shirt and blouse, can do better work than in garments grimy with dirt and grease. People who do not handle dirt have, of course, no excuse for being unclean. There is also unnoticed benefit in occasional change of the outer garments. It rejuvenates a suit of clothing or a dress to hang it in good air a day or two. The mind of the wearer in turn gets a fresh feeling by donning different clothing, or by varying the combination. Even a fresh necktie or polished shoes make a man feel new for an hour, and that is eminently worth the while. Few people are dandies or flirts; hence a flower on the person every day would minister to self-respect and a high-toned consciousness, having a direct bearing upon the soul's power of Will. A handkerchief touched with a bit of perfumery, though it be a red bandana in a mechanic's hands, would serve a similar purpose. Let fools laugh! A good Will has no care for asses' braying. A real man need be neither a prig nor a boor.

"It is related of Haydn, the musician, that, when he sat down to compose, he always dressed himself with the utmost care, had his hair nicely powdered, and put on his best suit. Frederick II had given him a diamond ring; and Haydn declared that, if he happened to begin without it, he could not summon a single idea. He could write only on the finest paper; and was as particular in forming his notes, as if he had been engraving them on copper-plate."

Rule 11. Similarly as to good music. "Take a music-bath once or twice a week for a few seasons," said Dr O.W. Holmes, "and you will find that is to the soul what the water-bath is to the body." This elevates and tends to maintain the tone of one's mind. Seek, therefore, every clean opportunity for hearing it. Purchase some kind of instrument for the home, and see that its beneficent harmonies are often heard. Let music be as much a part of the day's routine as eating or reading or working.

Rule 12. Discard, resolutely and forever everything thought to be injurious to health.

Rule 13. Always and everywhere cultivate high mindedness. Maintain the resolute Mood of Will. Assert yourself, for every good influence, against every evil thing. Carry with you in all activities the sense of nobility, of health, of success.

Rule 14. It should now be added that beyond dispute, personal power for maintaining and securing health is not confined to mere Will as is commonly understood. Below all moods of cheerfulness, hope, courage and Will—in ordinary thought—hides a dynamic psychic force which is capable even of "miracles", and which will ultimately rid the earth of disease and death. This psychic force is expressed partly in mental thought, but more perfectly and prophetically in a psychic state which is a complex of assumption, assertion, Will or sovereign authority—an idea of command in action conquering illness and securing health—and confidence and profound realization—that is, thought-feeling of betterment.

The path leading to such state is that of expecting effort to feel the state within the inner center of person. One should affirm that universal good is pouring in; one should assume and assert the fact; one should assume and assert that the ground of one's existence is the Infinite Reality, that one has deeply imbedded in the deeps of soul the idea of self as whole because the Infinite Ground does not and cannot wish otherwise, and that as the universal good enters from without and the Infinite Self emerges from below up into the subconscious personal self, all inharmonious conditions are necessarily passing away—being expelled.

The process above suggested cannot be acquired by brief and haphazard efforts. The soul must essay the process again and again until it discovers the process. Thereafter, it must put the process into action incessantly until facility and power in its use are acquired.

But observe: In real illness, *call your physician* and at the same time *bring your psychic power into requisition.* The notion that the physician and psycho-auto treatment are inconsistent and antagonistic is utterly false. Do not omit either method. Rise to the highest level of a free use of anything under heaven which helps life to health.

Make all the above suggestions a perpetual regime of your life.

"ATTENTION! I RESOLVE TO WILL!"

PART III

MENTAL REGIME

CHAPTER XVI

EXERCISES IN ATTENTION

It is subject to the superior authority of the Ego. I yield it or I withhold it as I please; I direct it in turn to several points; I concentrate it upon each point as long as my Will can stand the effort.

—"Dictionnaire Philosophique"
(Philosophical Dictionary)

Theory of Chapter

Attention, become habituated, involves constant and strong action of Will;
The idea of Willpower, always present in the effort to habituate attention, will come to possess and dominate the mind;
Such domination, by a psychic law, develops the function which it concerns.

The preceding chapters have had in view the development of Will by means of physical exercises. If the suggestions hitherto given have been followed, self-culture has resulted with marked growth in this direction. While our work has been physical, the mind has nevertheless been directly involved, for always the Will has thrust itself forward, both as ruler and as object. We are now to enter more particularly the mental field, with the same end in view.

Regimes

Exercise No. 1. Sit quietly at ease in a room where you will not be disturbed. By a supreme effort of Will, drive every thought and fancy out of your mind. Hold the mind blank as long as possible. How long can you sustain this effort successfully? Be not discouraged. Persistence will win. After a genuine attempt, rest for a few moments. Then try again. Practise the exercise daily for ten days, with rest of two days, making at least six attempts each day. Keep a record of the results, and at the end of the period, note the improvement made. The Will must be taught to be supreme.

Exercise No. 2. Sit quietly as before. When the mind is a blank, hold it so for a few seconds. Then instantly begin to think of a single thing, and now exclude every other thought. Keep the attention rigidly upon this particular subject as long as possible. The direction does not mean that you are to follow a train of ideas upon the subject, but that you are to fasten the mind keenly upon the one thing or idea and retain it in the field of attention, just as you may look at some object, focusing sight and observation there, and there alone. Rest. Repeat six times. Make record. Continue every day for ten days, with rest. Then note the improvement in power.

Exercise No. 3. Permit the mind to wander for one minute. Now write out all that you recall of these wandering thoughts. Then proceed to find and indicate in writing the connections that bind them into a chain. You will thus discover that mental activities may become aimless, but that the mind's roaming is not without explanation. Resolve to keep your thoughts well in hand. Repeat these exercises six times, and continue for ten days, with rest. On the tenth day, compare the records and note the improvement in attention. Try, now, to discover any general laws that have governed the mind's uncontrolled action.

Exercise No. 4. Sit at ease for one minute while thinking of the mind as engaged in reasoning. Do not entertain fancies. Keep out wandering thoughts and sensations. Do not reason; think of the reasoning power of the mind. Now, deliberately pursue some definite line of reasoning for, say, five minutes. Write the results, from memory. Rest. Repeat six times. Continue for ten days, with rest. On the tenth day, compare the records and note the improvement in concentration.

Repeat these exercises with the imagination, thinking of a picture or plot of acting.

Repeat with the power of Will, imagined as to various acts.

Exercise No. 5. Summons a resolute state of mind. Now, select some desired goal in life which you believe to be possible, and will, with all your might, that this shall be. Do not think of means. Fiercely resolve to overcome all difficulties. Do not dwell upon the enjoyment of success, for that will distract the mind. Attend wholly to the Mood of willing. Repeat six times. Continue for at least ten days, with rest.

Embed the idea of the goal deeply in mind. Carry it with you into life's activities. Make the resolution a permanent matter, not only of Will, but of feeling as well.

Exercise No. 6. Sit at ease for a few seconds. Now, think of several acts, as, to walk across the room, or to take a book from a shelf, or to sit still. Continue for about five minutes. Various impulses will arise to do one thing or another. Resist them all for a little time. Now decide, quickly and resolutely, what you will do. Do not act lazily; do not decide impulsively. Force a real decision. Then act. Do exactly that one thing. Rest. Repeat six times, with different actions. During each act, put the Will into every part thereof. Keep to the fore a strong personal Mood. Continue for ten days, with rest. At the end of the period, note improvement in attention and power of Will.

Exercise No. 7. Set apart by themselves several small objects; books, coins, paper-knives, etc. Collect a miscellaneous lot. Now, after looking at these articles over, decide to arrange them in some particular way according to a determined order of relations. The order may be that of similarity, or difference, and the like. Example: the objects are of many colors; arrange in a complementary way. Now note the general effect. It is probably bad. Why is this? How can the arrangement be improved? Has color anything to do with the arrangement of the furniture of your room? Can it be set into better order in this respect? Try that. Repeat with order according to other resemblances. Repeat with order according to differences.

Always keep the Mood of Will in the foreground during these exercises.

Arrange with a different order six times in each exercise. Continue for ten days, with rest. At the end of the period, observe improvement in attention, together with facility in making the arrangements.

Exercise No. 8. Select several like objects, say, books or articles of furniture. Now arrange the books according to titles. Is this the best possible arrangement? Try to improve it. Arrange the furniture for finest effect in the room, having color, shape, style, etc., in mind. Repeat with other similar articles. With each set of objects make six different arrangements. Continue for ten days, with rest. Then note the improvement as before.

Exercise No. 9. Select several dissimilar objects. Lay them out conveniently before you. Take one of them in hand. What does it suggest? Connect that suggestion immediately, that is, without any intermediate idea, with another article. What does this suggest? Connect the suggestion with a third article. Continue in this way until all the objects have been connected. Place the articles, one after another, according to connecting suggestions, before you. Do everything slowly, deliberately and with a strong sense of willing. Rest after the first complete experiment a few seconds. Then repeat with different articles six times. Continue for ten days, with rest, and then note improvement in attention and facility of connections made.

Here is an example: Book — (suggesting) — Person — (suggesting) — Note — (suggesting) — Writer — (suggesting) — Pen — (suggesting) — Mightier — (suggesting) — Sword (suggesting) — Sharp — (suggesting) — Knife — (suggesting) — Point — (suggesting) — Pin — (suggesting) — Bright— (suggesting) — Gold Watch.

The above exercises are somewhat difficult, and their practise will require patience and time. But the value of such work will appear when we remember "that the act of voluntary attention involves a conscious effort of the soul." It is the "*conscious effort*" that this book seeks to develop. And for two reasons: first, that the reader may acquire the habit of carrying with him everywhere the Will-pervaded Mood of the strong personality; secondly, that adequate power of attending to motives may become a permanent factor of his life.

Read, therefore, the following with greatest care: "*Variations in the relative strength of motives mainly arise from the degree of attention that we give to them respectively.*" People often act wrongly or unwisely because they fail here. "*Thus, for example, a hungry man, seeing bread in a baker's window, is tempted to break the glass and steal a loaf of bread. The motive here is the prospect of satisfying his hunger. But the man is not a mere machine, impelled by a single force. He knows that if he is caught, he will be punished as a thief. He knows, too, that this is a wrong act which he is considering, and that his conscience will reprove him. Now he can fix his attention upon one of these restraining motives. The impulse to break the glass thus loses its power. The element of time is an important factor, for the longer he delays and deliberates, the more numerous will be the restraining motives which arise in his consciousness.*"

But avoidance of crime is a very small part of most people's lives. For the majority, "How to get on in all good ways," is a comprehensive, and the ruling, question. The value of attention obtains here in ways similar to those above suggested. A strong

Will is demanded. Ability to hold the mind to one thing is imperative. Power of concentrating thought upon motives, and the best motives, is called for every day of our existence. The great symbol of all our exercises, therefore, is Attention! ATTENTION!

"From what has already been said, it can be inferred that tenacious attention is one of the strongest factors in a cultivated will. Some modern psychologists insist that attention is the only power of the will.

"The man who can hold uninteresting ideas before his mind until they gather interest, is the man who is going to succeed.

"The only way to cultivate attention is by a *continuous* effort of will. If the attention wanders from any subject for ninety-nine consecutive times, bring the attention back ninety-nine consecutive times. Make an effort to concentrate the mental powers each time. A habit of attention will surely grow in this way.

"It is hardly possible to overestimate the importance of tenacious attention. A man with half the natural ability of some geniuses often accomplishes far more, because he keeps his attention undivided on one thing until he has mastered it."

Here is an open secret of big, shrewd, notable men in the professional and financial marts of today—close, concentrated, calm-minded attention. It does not require a tight-fisted, muscle-tensed, set condition of body but rather a ONE AIM held closely in mind with distracting outside sensations excluded.

But the words which we have so often met in the preceding pages indicate the ultimate and priceless goal:

"I RESOLVE TO WILL! THE MOOD OF EMPHATIC PERSONALITY IS MINE!

CHAPTER XVII

ATTENTION IN READING

A distinguished lawyer of an Eastern city relates that while engaged in an argument upon which vast issues depended, he suddenly realized that he had forgotten to guard a most important point. In that hour of excitement, his faculties became greatly stimulated. Decisions, authorities and precedents long since forgotten began to return to his mind. Dimly outlined at first, they slowly grew plain, until at length he read them with perfect distinctness. Mr Beecher had a similar experience when he fronted the mob in Liverpool. He said that all events, arguments and appeals that he had ever heard or read or written passed before his mind as oratorical weapons, and standing there, he had but to reach forth his hand and seize the weapons as they went smoking by.

—Newell Dwight Hillis

Theory of Chapter

Concentrated attention the price of understanding;
Exhaustive understanding the only true reading;
Review and discussion the storing methods of memory;
These exercises, deliberately and persistently followed, are sure developers of the scholar's Will.

"Read not to contradict nor to believe, but to weigh and consider," said the wise and "woodeny" Bacon. "To weigh and consider"—that is the *open sesame* of right reading. In order to acquire these abilities, the following directions will serve:

Regimes

Exercise No. 1. Procure any well-written book on any subject worth knowing. Read the title with great care. State in your own language exactly what you suppose the title to mean. Look up the definitions of all words. Examples: "History of the United States". What is history? What is a written history? What is the difference between the two kinds of "history"? What is the main idea in "United States"? How did this name originate?

Now read the author's name. Before proceeding further, memorize an outline of his life. Ascertain his place in letters. What value are you to put upon his work?

This done, read with some care the table of contents. You ought now to have the general drift of the book, together with its purpose. If these do not appear, take another book and repeat the above exercises. Continue this exercise during life.

Exercise No. 2. Presuming that, with such examination, you wish to go on, read the preface very carefully. Having finished it, ask yourself what the author has here said. Make sure that you know. Then ask, Why has he said this in the preface? Did he need a preface? Does this preface really pre-face, so far as you can now judge? Make this a permanent regime in reading.

Exercise No. 3. If the book has an introduction, read that with the greatest attention. An author is sometimes misunderstood in many pages because his introduction has not been read. At the end of its reading, outline from memory what it has brought before you. Now ask, again, Why should he have written that introduction, or what he has written here as an introduction? Very likely, you are at this time as ready to lay the book aside as you may become later. Make this exercise a permanent part of serious reading.

Exercise 4. To make sure about this, read attentively the first twenty-five pages of the book. In these pages, do you see anything new, anything interesting, anything of value to you? If nothing new, interesting or valuable gets to the fore in twenty-five pages, you are probably ready to sell that book at a large discount. The rule, however, is not infallible. Reading is frequently like gold-mining: the richest veins are not always readily discovered. Some of George Eliot's works require a yoke of oxen, so to speak, to drag the mind into them; but once in, it cannot escape her spell. Many books which are perennially acknowledged cannot be rigidly subjected to these tests. Something, too, depends upon the reader's mind. If the mind "adores" "awfully sweet" dresses and "perfectly elegant" parties, its judgments may be taken with a "lot" of "just the tiniest" allowance. These directions are not dealing with the "punk" order of intellect, nor the "green corn" era of criticism. They have in view the ordinary run of minds and the above-average grade of books. If twenty-five pages of a book do not get hold of a good mind, the author has done phenomenally fine work, or else he isn't worth reading. Make this exercise permanent.

Exercise No. 5. Supposing, now, that you resolve to go on with the volume in hand, it will be necessary, for our present purpose, to return to the first sentence. Read that sentence with exceeding care. What is its subject?—its predicate?—its object? What is the meaning of each word? If an abstract-thought, put this thought into your own language. Think it, resolutely and carefully and clearly. If it is an object-thought, stop now, and, closing the eyes, call up a mental picture of the object. If the word expresses action, ask what kind of action. Think the act so as to get a mental picture of it, if possible. If the sentence is involved, take as much of it as expresses a complete thought exhausted by ideas of "being", or "condition", or "action". Treat this as your first sentence according to the above directions. Then proceed with the next complete thought of the sentence, and so on until you have in this manner read the sentence as a whole. Then read the sentence again, put the thoughts together, and get into the mind a complete view of the entire statement. Always translate the author's thoughts into your own language. *Do not memorise, but* THINK.

Proceed in this way through the first paragraph. Then, state in your own manner the connected chain of thought thus far presented.

The next day, write, without reading again, the substance of this first paragraph.

Continue such attentive and analytic reading until you have mastered the first chapter. Now, put aside all writings hitherto made, and from memory write a connected statement of the substance of that chapter.

Proceed with the succeeding sentences, paragraphs and chapters. If these directions are pursued, few books will require a second reading. And one good book well read is better than a dozen read, as books ordinarily are read.

Resolve permanently upon this kind of reading.

Such exercises will prove of immense value, because they are based on certain laws of mind. The eye acquires great facility in reading, and the reader is apt to content himself with whole but vague pictures of groups of ideas presented. In order that the thought contained in the printed page may be really obtained, it is necessary to break up these wholes and to put their parts into clear light. This requires attention to details, which in turn demands a distinct understanding of the meaning of words. We may catch the general thought of a sentence without knowing clearly what some of its words mean, and thus really miss, perhaps, the best part of our reading.

"Suppose I look out of my window," says Hill in "Elements of Psychology", "and see a black horse running swiftly. The whole picture, as presented by the sense of vision, constitutes one single image. It remains one and single until I have occasion to describe it in words. The moment I attempt to do so, an analytic process or process of resolution into parts is necessary. I must name the animal 'horse', his color 'black', his act 'running', his speed 'swiftly', and I must indicate whether it is a definite or an indefinite black horse that runs, and so must use an article, 'a' or 'the'. Putting all together, I say '*A black horse is running swiftly,*' a sentence in which my one visual image is broken up by five distinctions, each expressed in a separate word. There is truth in the proverb, 'No one knows a thing until he can tell it'."

The object of putting thought into one's own words is also seen in the fact that the mere study of words, as the above writer indicates, is of little value. Hence in real reading, it is always necessary to secure mental images, or mental conceptions clear-cut and pronounced, of "being", "condition" or "action" involved in each statement read.

Exercise No. 6. While reading any book worth the while, mark striking or useful passages, and, as you proceed, make an index on the rear fly leaf. No matter if the book has a printed index; your own will prove better for your purpose.

Exercise No. 7. Analyze chapters, about as you go on, and mark and number or letter the points made. At the close of reading the chapter, review these points and fix in memory. This will facilitate Exercise No. 5.

Exercise No. 8. While some friend reads aloud, practise mental noting of the points made by the author, retaining them for a given number of pages. Then state them consecutively while the reader reviews to correct your errors. Continue this exercise indefinitely.

Exercise No. 9. Repeat the above exercise with conversations with the reader, making sure that both thoroughly understand the matter in hand. On the following day, review this work together from memory. Then continue as before. Practise these exercises indefinitely.

Exercise No. 10. If an author's name is not a sufficient guaranty for his statements, or if his book is written from an evident point of view or with a possible bias, and he is clearly bent on "making his case", bring to the reading of his work the interrogative attitude of the mind. Do not accept him carelessly. Compel him to "make his case" fairly. Verify his alleged facts. See that his references are correct and rightly interpreted. Detect flaws in his arguments. Read him from his point of view as modified by your own. Make sure that your point of view is good. Therefore, be open to his convictions. Nevertheless, antagonize him in a fair field. Be not hasty to contradict, nor to surrender. Tomorrow what you deny may be the truth, what you accept may be false. Read resolutely to gather what he can contribute to your stock of facts, of realities, of sound reasoning, of sentiment, of life, of power.

In connection with the foregoing instructions on attention in reading, certain parts of Bacon's essay "On Studies" will be of interest:

"Studies serve for delight, for ornament, and for ability. Their chief use for delight is in privateness and retiring; for ornament, is in discourse; and for ability, is in the judgment and disposition of business. For expert men can execute, and perhaps judge of particulars, one by one; but the general counsels, and the plots and the marshalling of affairs, come best from those who are learned. ...Crafty men condemn studies; simple men admire them; *and wise men use them.* ...Read not to contradict and confuse; nor to believe and take for granted; nor to find talk and discourse, but to weigh and consider. Histories make men wise; poets witty; the mathematics subtle; natural philosophy deep; moral grave; logic and rhetoric able to contend.

"Reading maketh a full man; conference a ready man; and writing an exact man. And therefore, if a man write little, he had need have a great memory; if he confer little, he had need have a present wit; and if he read little, he had need have much cunning, to seem to know that he doth not."

Beware what Ben Jonson called a "humor":

> "A Humour is the bias of the mind,
> By which, with violence, 'tis one way inclined;
> It makes our action lean on one side still;
> And, in all changes, *that way bends the Will.*"

The work here suggested will be tedious at first, and it demands time and patience. As it proceeds, however, it will become more and more easy and delightful. Its justification is the double purpose in hand in all these pages: right reading and power of persistent Will. *A resolute sense of willing must, therefore, be preserved from first to last.* Learn to read in the Mood of the emphatic personality. Your Will shall then dissolve books, and mastered books shall culture the finest Will.

CHAPTER XVIII

ATTENTION IN THINKING

Something more reliable than a mere impulse is needed to make a strong mind. Back of all must stand a strong Will, with the ability and disposition to use it. M. Marcel well says, 'The great secret of education lies in exciting and directing the Will.' In later mental acquirements, we recognize the omnipotence of Will. Nothing takes its place until we discover that attention is under the control of the Will, and until, by perseverance, we acquire the power of thus controlling it.

—"Popular Science Monthly"

Theory of Chapter

True thinking is a deliberative act of mind held fast to its task;
Such impelled action discovers the best use of mind, and develops and stores the whole man;
The mind thus improved throws itself into its operations with greater wisdom and increased energy;
This action unfolds the Will.

The best thinker is the best reader. This is true even of "reciters", so far as their work is concerned. To recite, one must interpret; to interpret, one must think.

Thinking, in its noblest sense, is largely a lost art among the people. They indulge in a vast deal of mental jargon, but genuine thought seems a scarce article. A single "straw" is the fact that new matter presented in the simplest language is often declared to be "too deep for us". The difficulty is not depth, but unfamiliarity; the limits of popular thinking are narrow; outside these limits, even sunlight is opaque, and diamonds are mere quartz pebbles.

People "think", as they say, to be sure, concerning homes, business, politics, social and state affairs, together with a smattering of religion; but in an elevated way, this "thinking" is a good deal like the "thinking" of animals; vague, unconscious as thought, forced, disjointed, spasmodic, haphazard. Few seem to think out a great reality, build up a consistent theory, or elaborate a reasonable system. We have not here, altogether, it must be said, the pressure of dirt and moil. It is a case of mental laziness. One must work with muscles in order to exist; but one need not labor with the mind for assimilation of food and development of brawn. House-keepers and shop-tenders aver a great amount of thinking, "real and wearisome"; but we have here very largely the mechanics of mental routine. The world is flooded with "literature" every day, and the most of its readers relax in its enervating tide. Evidence: few "get on", few discover themselves and the universe about them—infinite globe of dynamic influences for the elevation of the human soul.

Regimes

Exercise No. 1. Take now, any simple and great truth. Concentrate attention upon this truth, absolutely excluding every other thought. Example: "Man is immortal". Think of man as immortal only. Think of man in every conceivable way as being immortal. Man is body; what is body? Is body immortal? Is *the* body immortal? If not, in either case, why not? If so, in either case, why? And in what sense? Man has mind; what is mind? Is it immortal? If so, what in mind is immortal? Why do you believe as you do? If mind is immortal, for what purpose? Man, again, has moral consciousness. What is this? Is this immortal? In what sense? What in moral consciousness is immortal? Why do you so believe? For what purpose is man, as moral consciousness, immortal?

Now think of immortality. What is it? Think of immortality in every conceivable way as connected with man. How does it concern him? Has it various supposable or believable states in relation to him? Where is he, as you suppose, in immortality? What is he, according to your idea, to become in immortality? What is he to take with him at death? With whom is he to exist hereafter? What is he to do? What relation have his present states to any believable states of his future life? How does he get his idea of immortality? What purpose does the idea serve in his life? In your life? Why should man be immortal?

When thinking of *man,* always keep in mind the idea "immortal", and when thinking of *immortality,* always keep in mind the idea "man".

The above is merely an example. These exercises should be repeated every day, with a different sentence or thought, indefinitely. It will be well also to preserve dated records, and to make frequent comparisons in order to discover improvement in analysis, attention and power of persistent thought upon a single subject. In six months, profit and pleasure will be apparent. You will surely find, as the main result of a faithful compliance with all suggestions, a tremendous power of straightforward Will-action. There can be no failure with resolute practise.

Exercise No. 2. Take any simple matter of observation or experience. You are riding, let us suppose, along a country road. Now look well at the landscape. You pronounce it beautiful. But what is the beautiful? Think that question to an answer. Now bury your mind in deepest thought concerning the landscape before you. The landscape—"what is *a* landscape?" Think that subject out carefully and distinctly. Proceeding, ask, "What is *this* landscape?" Observe the general outlines and salient features. What is there about the larger details which makes them beautiful? Observe the minor details. What is their beauty?

How do they contribute to the beauty of the whole? How might this landscape be improved in beauty? How would this or that change add to the effect of the beautiful? Have you discovered all elements before you of a beautiful nature? When you next ride over the road, remember that question. Are you familiar with this country? Was it ever more beautiful than it is today? Do other people declare it to be beautiful? If not, why not, in your opinion? Ah! But are you certain that your ideas of the beautiful are correct? Do you think that the elements of this landscape appeal in the same way to others who pronounce it beautiful as they appeal to you? Do you suppose that they observe just the same colors, outlines, proportions, contrasts and blendings as yourself? Do you believe that the same feelings, thoughts, moods and desires are awakened in their minds by this landscape as in your own?

By such a process, you may become absorbed in a deliberate and controlled train of thoughts. If you have followed these directions, you have had experience in perfect concentration.

Concentration is the secret of great thinking.

This exercise should be varied at every attempt, with different subjects, as opportunity may present. It must be continued six months at least, and practised in some suggested way every day.

Exercise No. 3. Take any simple sentence, say, "Success in life depends upon nobility of purpose and persistence of effort." Write the sentence out in full. Now strip the statement to a mere skeleton: "Success — depends — purpose — effort." Think clearly the meaning of each word. Then imagine the modifying words placed just above these. The sentence will read:

"Life—nobility—persistence."
"Success—depends—purpose—effort."

You have now two skeletons which may be filled out at your liking, almost, and yet give you the same idea in essentials. "The value of life consists in its nobility and its persistence." This sentence suggests the meaning of true success. That is not success which has no nobility or persistence. So, the lower skeleton may be filled out to read: "The quality of success depends upon the quality and abiding nature of its purpose and its effort." Low purpose and effort, low grade of success. Thus, the "value of life consists in its nobility of purpose and its persistence of effort."

Continue this exercise with different sentences for six months.

Exercise No. 4. Write the sentence used in the preceding exercise, as an example. "Success in life depends upon nobility of purpose and persistence of effort." Now ask the first part of this sentence closing with "purpose", a series of questions in which the words "how", "why", "which", "when", "where", "whose", are employed. "*How* does success depend upon nobility of purpose?" "*Why* does success in life depend upon nobility of purpose?" "*What* success depends upon nobility of purpose?" "*Where* does success depend upon nobility of purpose?" And so on until all the words are used. Write each answer in full. Then substitute "persistence of effort" for "nobility of purpose", and bombard the statement again with the same questions. Write each answer in the latter case in full. Then ask the entire sentence a question containing the word "whose". Finally, note carefully all that you have written upon the statement, arrange in logical form, and proceed to write a simple essay with the material thus gathered. You will find this to be an excellent way in which to bore into any subject. Continue six months, at least.

This is merely an example, and it is not a very full one. Every word and proposition of a sentence or subject thus may be compelled to give up its contents. In time, too, the mind will have acquired great facility and power in such analysis, so that whatever of value is read will come to offer its secrets to you almost as a free gift. This alone is worth all labor expended upon the exercise.

Exercise No. 5. The results of attention and concentration will very nearly approach composition. Everyone who thinks can write, at least after a fashion. Writing is one of the best of aids to thinking. When you attempt to write, you discover, very likely, that what you supposed you knew has been apprehended in the vaguest manner.

Take, therefore, any object, fact, truth, law or proposition. Example: the law or force of gravitation. Now ask as many questions as possible concerning this fact. Bombard it with "what", "whose", "why", "where", "when", "how", "with what conditions", "how long", and the like. Thus: What is it? Whose is it? Where is it? When is it? How is it? etc., until you have exhausted your power of thought upon it. Turn it about. Look at it from every side. Examine it under all conditions. Find its nature, its operation, its source, its purpose, its bearing upon other natural forces. Ravel it out. Tear it into pieces. Write all answers in full. Then proceed to arrange all answers in groups after some logical order. Now read the material thus arranged, and you will discover new thought springing up, which will necessitate a rearrangement. Write this in full. Then fill out your synopsis in the best manner possible. Continue this exercise frequently for six months.

Meanwhile, study the cleanest and clearest writers for details of expression and correctness of statement and form. Review your work occasionally, and note the improvement, both in composition and ability to get into a subject. Keep the ideal of straightforward simplicity always in mind. Declare war upon superlatives, and reduce your adjectives two-thirds. In all cases, use the fewest words consistent with clean statements and full expression.

Exercise No. 6. Proceed as in former exercise to completion of synopsis. Now think this out, fully and clearly, as written. Memorize the thoughts, but never the words, section by section, taking several days if necessary, until the entire subject lies in your mind ready to be spoken or written in full. In doing this, you must *think in words.* Let the purpose in mind be to speak the thoughts as if to an audience. When you are master of the subject, speak all your thoughts in order to an imaginary gathering of people. Have the audience before you. Be in earnest. Get excited. Over the law of gravity? Certainly. Over anything under the heavens! Make gestures. Fear nothing. Never mind mistakes. Be keenly alive to this piece of work. Forget every other reality in the world. You believe certain things in connection with the law; deliver your soul on that matter as if to an audience of people who never have heard of it or do not think as you do.

This exercise should be continued for many months. A few moments devoted to it each day will prove of incalculable value. Almost any real subject will answer for a topic. Business, Politics, Farming, Magazines. After some experience, it will be well to avoid general topics and to select those of a narrower range, as, The Tides, The Party, The Raising of Celery, The Liquefaction of Air, etc.

Exercise No. 7. Study unceasingly to detect errors in your own thinking. Are your main propositions correct? Do you employ right words in stating them? Are the conclusions really deducible from your propositions? Why do you believe certain things? Are they based on actual facts? Are the facts sufficiently numerous to form a basis for belief? Are you biased in examination of facts? Do you think as you do because of desire, or ignorance, or prejudice? Make sure of your facts! Make sure that the facts prove one thing, and none other!

Exercise No. 8. Follow the above suggestions as to the thinking of other people. They are swearing by a host of things which are not necessarily so. Do not become a bore, nor a judge. But make sure that arguments actually prove matters as asserted.

This chapter may well close with a quotation, taken from the author's published work, "*The Culture of Courage*", concerning mental health.

"When the mental attitude concerns truth, the mind is sanely intelligent, and, in the long run, will exhibit reasonableness.

"Any illustration of the attitude will be more or less incomplete, because the process unfolded uncovers so much of life. It should, therefore, be remembered that the following are merely specimen leaves from the vast forest of experience.

"*Illustration No. 1.* A man sees a ghost in the highway. Our invitation requires that he see the fact as it is. It is *some* fact; what *is* that fact? It is a tall stump with two or three naked branches, various lights and shadows moving upon them. The fact-*thing* has now become a fact-*group.* It is an appearance—a fact suggesting a supposed truth. What was the *real* truth? The ghostly body was a stump, the arms were branches, the movements were due to flickering shadows and varying degrees of light. The supposed truth was a ghost. The real truth was a mental deception; back of that a stump under certain conditions.

"Ten thousand applications are possible. I take one only—cures of all sorts of disease attributed to all sorts of remedies. We need not deny the cures; there are millions of cures, blessed be Nature! But is the agency of cure in any given case precisely what it is said to be? Is this the ghost fact of Christian Science, Mental Healing, drugs, or prayer? All the things named contain values for us. I simply suggest that when you attribute your cure to one agency or another, you strip all claims down to the naked fact. That is the one sane test of the question whether a thing is a ghost or a fact.

"*Illustration No. 2.* Witchcraft had its facts, its supposed truth, and—its real truth. When men insisted on seeing the real facts, many of the fictitious facts disappeared, the supposed truth vanished, and the real truth—awaited discovery. After science had adopted the above methods, instead of the old shout, 'superstition'—contentment in which has hurt science more than it has hurt any other department of our life—the backlying facts began to emerge, and the truths, clairvoyance, clairaudience, hypnotism, fear, imagination, etc., came slowly into light. We are now trying to find out why science should say, 'all bosh' to 'mesmerism', 'occultism', spiritualism, religion, or any other thing under the heavens."

The conclusion is this: Make sure of the facts; get at the real truth; keep open house to every proposition claiming to be real, but accept nothing not clearly demonstrated to sane but inspired reason.

The purpose of these studies on attention in thinking is to train you to establish the habit of knowing all sides of any question that confronts you; to observe all possibilities and consequences attendant upon your decision to "do this" or "do that." "Those who have not early been trained to see all sides of a question are apt to be extremely narrow, and undesirable to live with."

However, the ferreting out and discovering all possible phases of any matter before you is but one part of the complete circle. Having "attended in thinking", and seeing the proper course to pursue—then must be brought forward the great jewel of ACTION in the line of best interest. "The world demands for success not only plenty of thought, but quickness of thought. More than half the world thinks after it is too late."

Become accustomed to deep, attentive thinking.

Always try to "think all around a subject".

Try and do the required thinking before you go "into the game".

Once clear thinking is done, *swiftly carry it into ACTION.*

In every part of the work of this chapter, keep in mind the sentence: "I am conscious of the sense of Will." You will not be distracted, but rather helped by that recollection.

"ONLY WILL! ALL THINGS ARE POSSIBLE TO HIM THAT WILLS."

CHAPTER XIX

Exercises in Memory

I retain a clear impression or image of everything at which I have looked, although the coloring of that impression is necessarily vivid in proportion to the degree of interest with which the object was regarded. I find this faculty of much use and solace to me. By its aid, I can live again, at will, in the midst of any scene or circumstances by which I have been surrounded. By a voluntary act of mind, I can in a moment conjure up the whole of any one out of the innumerable scenes in which the slightest interest has at any time been felt by me.

—Dr John Kitto

Theory of Chapter

Review deepens mental impressions;
Storing of mind enlarges it, and gives it immense momentum;
The effort to secure mental force multiplies Will-energy.

It was John Ruskin who said, "There are but two strong conquerors of the forgetfulness of men, Poetry and Architecture." But Ruskin had the far outlook in mind. There is but one strong conqueror of the personal forgetfulness, and that is the determined Will. The poem and the cathedral preserve their age in the world's memory; the resolute Will preserves the individual's mind from becoming a sieve. The Rev. Dwight Hillis once remarked in a lecture, that he forgot with his memory. This was an old pleasantry. Men forget at times because of the rush of thought forbidding the quick grasp of mind necessary to the thing desired. But the real secret of forgetting lies in a vaporous condition of Will.

Regimes

Exercise No. 1. Select the best specimen of condensed and simple English that you can find. Read a paragraph carefully. Begin to read again, defining to yourself every word. If you are in the slightest doubt, consult a dictionary. Go hungry a month to possess a first-class dictionary. After satisfying yourself that you understand every word in the first sentence, make sure that you understand the sentence as a whole. Now proceed, attentively and with strong Will, to repeat the first few words, keeping words and *thought* in mind. Do not repeat like a parrot, but think, resolving to remember—*the words and what they say.* Continue until you have memorized this part of the sentence. Then, go on in the same manner with the next few words. Fix these firmly in your mind. Now, recall all words and thought thus far committed, and repeat, again and again, thinking the thought as you do so with the utmost attention and energy. Proceed in this way until the entire sentence is mastered.

It will be better not to try too many words at a time; you will easily ascertain the number most convenient to your mind.

In this method, never for a moment forget to keep in mind the *ideas* presented by the language. As words often represent different shades of meaning, will attention to the shade here used. Let the work be done with the utmost concentrated energy.

If you will repeat that sentence frequently during the day, wherever you chance to be, *always thoughtfully and determinedly,* you will fasten it firmly in your mind.

If you will repeat the same exercise with another sentence the following day, and frequently repeat both sentences, the first will become more deeply impressed you're your memory, and the second will be acquired as fully as was the first.

The value of repetition is not new. But the point of this exercise lies not so much in repetition of words as in concentrated and continuous gripping of their thought. In all repetition, therefore, study and master the ideas which they present.

It may be supposed that you are memorizing some brief poem or bit of prose. When it has been acquired, you should frequently repeat it as a whole; say, once in several days, and later, once during several weeks. In a comparatively short time, it will have become indelibly stamped upon the mind. Two or three times a year thereafter recall it, which will preserve it from "drifting out" again.

Read originals now and then for correction of unconscious errors.

If it is the thought that you are mainly concerned about, use it as often as possible in conversation or writing; work it over in your own material; you will thus work it thoroughly into your own mind. This once done, words and source are of little importance. Here is plagiarism defensible before the gods. They, indeed, practise it more than their worshipers.

Some books are not worth much labor. There are others which will amply repay a resolve to master them. If you thoroughly master one small book during a year, as life and reading go, you will do well.

But there are few books that should be verbally memorized. You wish the contents rather than the words. These may be acquired in the following manner, supposing the book is not largely technical, and to a degree, perhaps, if it is so:

Exercise No. 2. First, know what the book treats. Now read a paragraph very carefully, making sure that you understand every word and its thought as a whole. Then, take the first complete statement of fact or theory, whether involving one sentence or many, and think it out aloud and in your own words. Read again, and restate the thought in different language from that employed by the author or by yourself in the effort just indicated. Imagine that you are speaking to some person; recite to him; compel him to listen; act as though trying to teach him. Seek opportunity to do the same with real people. Become, without ostentation, a walking instructor. Don't be a bore, but resolve to become the most interesting converser among your acquaintances. But remember, it is always the contents of that book that you are trying to make your own property.

In addition to the above, say to yourself frequently during the day: "This book affirms, at such and such a place, so and so"—stating where and what the matter is. Do this as often as it may be convenient. When you make this effort of memory, think backward and forward in the book from that point. At the close of the day, repeat all that you have thus far mastered. Then, read the book for correction of errors.

On the following day, repeat the same process with the next complete statement.

Continue as above until you have passed through an entire chapter.

Now, without reading, try to make in your mind alone a mere skeleton of the main thoughts of that chapter. Then memorize the skeleton. The chapter may reduce to one or two general statements, or it may involve a number of general together with subordinate propositions. Make these in their order your own.

When the skeleton has been firmly fixed in your mind, review from memory the series of statements already thought out and memorized, and of which the skeleton is a reduction. This will preserve the filling-in of the synopsis. Thereafter, at convenient intervals, proceed in a like manner, now to review the outline, now to recall the detailed propositions.

Now, proceed in the same way to the next chapter. Always think the written thoughts in your own words. Repeat during each day all preceding thought-statements of the chapter in hand, as well as the one of that day. When the second chapter has been finished, think out from memory a skeleton of its contents. Meanwhile, during the exercises with the present chapter, occasionally recall the thought-statements, in outline and in detail, of the first chapter, looking well after their order. When the second chapter has been acquired, think out occasionally a consecutive statement of the contents of both chapters. Then construct a new skeleton of all thoughts thus far presented, and memorize as an everlasting possession.

Continue until you have mastered the book.

In all this work, ignore whatever is not strictly essential to any sentence-thought, or to any statement-paragraph.

Such labor will tax your patience, but it will surely make you the master of your book, and will in time give you the greatest facility in reading. Ultimately, the mind may be depended upon to supply all necessary filling-in, if the skeletons have been well understood and thoroughly memorized. You will have acquired the ability, if your author is worth reading, when you know his general propositions, to think the details without further reading, unless the matter is technical or historical, or the like.

Exercise No. 3. While passing slowly through a room, glance swiftly and attentively around. Then, in another room, recall as many objects noted as may be possible. Do nothing languidly. Put your entire energy into this exercise. Repeat every day for ten days, with rest of two days, making a record of results. On the tenth day, compare records and note improvement.

Exercise No. 4. When on the street, note, as you pass along, all objects around you. Having passed a block, recall as many objects as possible. Repeat frequently every day. Repeat during ten days, with rest, and on the tenth day, note improvement.

Exercise No. 5. Resolve with great Willpower, when you retire, to awaken at a certain hour, and instantly to arise. If you fail for a time, be not discouraged; persevere and your mind will surely remember. But you must instantly arise at the appointed time, or your self will discover that you do not really mean what you profess to will. Continue until you have acquired the ability to awaken at any desired hour.

Exercise No. 6. In the morning, resolve to recall a certain thought at an exact hour. You must think mightily on this resolution and fix it firmly in your mind. Then dismiss it from immediate thought and attend to other duties as usual. Do not try to keep it in mind. In time, you will obey your own order. You will probably fail at first, but perseverance will make you master of appointments of this kind. The reflex influence in other matters will appear in due time. Continue for at least six months.

Exercise No. 7. When you start for your school or place of business, intensely resolve to return by a certain different route from that followed in going. Put your whole mind into this determination. In time, you will not fail to remember. Never by action contradict any of these resolutions. Continue for at least six months.

Exercise No. 8. Walk or drive to your school or place of business, and return home, in as many different and previously planned ways as possible. Never deviate from the plan. At the end of each, arrange another for going and coming, and adhere to it as a matter of the utmost importance. Continue for at least six months.

Exercise No. 9. At the beginning of each day make a plan for your general conduct until evening. Learn to have an order for action. Be the master of yourself. Having decided upon such a plan for the day, never, if possible to carry it out, vary its execution. Do not plan for more than one day at a time, unless the nature of your doings requires it, and in this event, leave particulars for each morning. Make your plans with care and strong Will, but do not burden the mind with them in a way to interfere with details that spring up. Command your mind to attend to the plan without forcing you to unnecessary strain of conscious thought. It is always better to arrange for results, leaving minute details to be decided according to demands of the moment. Continue for six months.

Exercise No. 10. At the close of each day, carefully review your thoughts and doings since morning. What have been your most valuable ideas? What are your most emphatic sensations? What are your most important actions? Have you carried out your plans? If not, then why? How have your thoughts, feelings and doings improved? What have been your motives? Have they been wise and worthy? Resolve upon betterment the next day, and incorporate this resolution into its plan. Continue this exercise indefinitely.

The preceding are suggestions only. They are based upon a law of the mind. If they appear to be unnecessary and tedious, that may be an evidence of the indeterminate and weak Will. It is a law, as remarked by Dr James Sully, "that *increase in the power of foreseeing action tends to widen the area of resolution.* Thus, so far as our daily actions become ordered according to a plan, they all have a stage of resolution as their antecedent. We habitually look forward to the succession of actions making up the business, etc., of the day, and resolve to perform them in due order as circumstances occur. And the subordination of action to ruling ends implies, as hinted above, a habitual state of resolution, that is preparedness to act in certain ways in certain circumstances".

Exercise No. 11. Make it a rule of life to learn some new and useful thing every day. Especially go outside of your business for such information. This will test the Will and store the memory.

Exercise No. 12. Frequently commit to memory lists of dates, and review often enough to hold in memory.

Make groupings of historic dates and commit them to memory. Link each group as a group with other groups from time to time. Frequently review.

Exercise No. 13. Make lists of objects of public interest in your community, with skeletons of information concerning them. Commit, and frequently review.

Exercise No. 14. Commit and frequently review lists of names, such as that of presidents, monarchs, and so on.

Exercise No. 15. Determine thoroughly to study some subject that lies outside your business. Keep at it. Remember, growth of mind and Will!

Exercise No. 16. Make the following a perpetual regime:

- Never be content with any partial acquaintance with things.
- Learn to refer items of knowledge to general principals.
- Employ all aids suggested by any particular study.
- Follow some natural or logical order in fixing facts, propositions, etc., in memory.
- Cultivate attentive observation wherever you are placed.
- Stand squarely and conscientiously on the side of truth.

CHAPTER XX

EXERCISES IN IMAGINATION

Whenever a person wills, or, rather, professes to will, to imagine, he has in fact already imagined; and, consequently, there can be no such thing as imaginations which are exclusively the result of a direct act of the Will.

—Professor Upham

I am inclined to think it was his practice, when engaged in the composition of any work, to excite his vein by the perusal of others on the same subject or plan, from which the slightest hint caught by his imagination, as he read, was sufficient to kindle there such a train of thought as, but for that spark (and that direction of the Will) had never been awakened.

—Sir Thomas Moore, "Life of Lord Byron"

Theory of Chapter

The highest imagination involves all the powers of the mind;
Willed culture of imagination secures its greatest efficiency;
The steadfast application of imagination highly cultured to the concerns of life requires the strongest and best-regulated exercise of Willpower;
That means the mighty Will developed all round.

"All the leaders in the world's life have been men of imagination."

It is in the action of the imagination that the question is presented, whether a man's life shall be governed by the subconscious mind to take him where it may, or by the conscious Will in control of that great servant. The imagination should be cultivated because it has so important a place in all our affairs, but its cultivation should always have reference to the sway of reason in conjunction with a reasonable Will. "The subjective mind," well said Olston in "Mind Power and Privileges", "will feed upon, and create, from the material given it by the Will." Schopenhauer said, "My mind draws its food from the medium of intelligence and thought; this nourishment gives body to my work." He, however, directed the course of his reading and thought to such things as would bear upon his general theme.

Our task in imagination, then, involves not only action of Will, but as well education of the deepest self in the interest of reason, judgment and right motives in life.

Regimes

Exercise No. 1. We begin, first, with simple imaginary sensations. Recall a single rose, and imagine its fragrance. Now, place yourself in mind before a hill of roses, and imagine the air to be heavy with their fragrance. What would be the effect upon yourself? What would you do in such a case? Repeat this exercise with a drop of musk. Then think of a lake of musk. Repeat with the notes of a song-bird. Then imagine a forest full of birds, all singing.

These exercises should be conducted in a quiet room. Bring the Will to bear with great power upon the work. Make the imagination as strong and distinct as possible. Repeat until the imaginary sensations become as vivid as in life.

Exercise No. 2. Stand by the side of some running stream, or near a waterfall, or in a factory in operation. Now listen attentively to the sounds that assail your ears. There is one general combination of sound. What is it like? What does it recall to memory? What mood does it bring to your soul? After you have become familiar with the whole effect, proceed to analyze it into as many different notes as you can detect. When you have done this thoroughly—have separated the whole sound into its component parts—imagine clearly and powerfully, a great volume of one of these sounds, making it as loud as possible; then continue with another, and a third, and so on, until the general combination has been exhausted.

Lastly, go away from a source of real sound to a quiet place, and recall, first the general harmony, and then its individual sounds as previously analyzed. Continue until the exercise may be carried on with perfect ease.

Exercise No. 3. Recall to memory some distant and real landscape. The difficulty will consist in bringing up the details, but these must be supplied. Resolute practise will accomplish the desired result. By a supreme effort make the mental picture as real as in life. In doing this, you should try to reinstate the soul's moods occasioned by the original scene. Place yourself, in thought, on the exact spot where first you saw the landscape, and resolutely compel the view to rise before you with as much of detail as possible. Keep the willful mood, and continue with different landscapes until you can summon a vivid picture of real scenery with the greatest ease.

Exercise No. 4. Recall some experience which has made a lasting impression upon your memory. Pass again in thought through its various phases, slowly, carefully, with great intensity of feeling. Dwell upon its cause, its accessories, and its effect upon you at the time. Was the effect pleasant or otherwise? In either case, state why. What influence had it upon your subsequent life? Would you repeat it? If not, then why? If so, may it again be secured—and how? May it be avoided in the future—and how?

Continue with various experiences until the lessons of caution and thoughtful self-interest become permanent factors in your mind.

Exercise No. 5. In a quiet room, construct imaginary pictures, such as you have never seen: —of a bird, grotesque and unreal; of an animal, curious yet beautiful, or perfectly tame but horrible; of a building, magnificent yet mysterious; of a landscape, weird and entrancing or wild but not forbidding. Do not allow the mind to wander into reverie. You should preserve the Will-mood as strongly as possible. Continue until control of the imagination has been secured.

Exercise No. 6. Gaze at some large object, and try to discover in or about it a suggestion for the play of imagination. Is it a horse? Give it wings, and journey to a distant planet. Is it a spool of thread? Make it to be a spider's web wherewith to weave a thousand robes or with which to send messages without unwinding by charging with intensest Willpower as you breathe upon it. Continue with other objects and various fanciful imaginings until Will is the master of imagination—to call up, to control or to banish.

Exercise No. 7. Select a sentence from a standard author, which illustrates the celerity of a trained imagination, and then will into the mind the complete picture suggested. Thus, Lowell, in "A Moosehead Journal", writes: "Sometimes a root-fence stretched up its bleaching antlers, like the trophies of a giant hunter." The man who said this tells us that "the divine faculty is to *see* what everybody can *look at*." The "divine faculty: of "*seeing*" should be cultivated. And it may become an Aladdin's Lamp to him whose Will is mighty. Try, now, to picture this root-fence of Lowell's scene in such a way as to suggest bleaching antlers. Why did the writer bleach the antlers? Why did he not see them poised upon a row of deer-heads?

Or, take another sentence from the same author: "A string of five loons was flying back and forth in long, irregular zigzags, uttering at intervals their wild, tremulous cry, which always seems far away, like the last faint pulse of echo dying among the hills, and which is one of those few sounds that, instead of disturbing solitude, only deepen and confirm it." Now, if you have not heard the cry of the loon, try to imagine a sound which reminds you of "the last faint pulse of echo dying among the hills." If you have heard these birds, call up the scene and its impressions as vividly as possible. In either case, make the present impression absolutely real. Keep the mind from wandering, holding it to the mood suggested. Then resolutely banish scene and feeling.

Having ascertained what the imaginative element is in such sentences (you can find similar everywhere), proceed to write some statement in which a like play of fancy is obtained. Do not be discouraged. Throw yourself into the mood of imagination. Practise this entire exercise persistently until you can with ease secure the mood and write a sentence of imaginative beauty.

The old injunction, "Know thyself", is by most people sadly neglected. It is worth a deal of labor to get acquainted with this "unknown land". Lowell writes that "a man should have traveled thoroughly round himself and the great *terra incognita* just outside and inside his own threshold, before he undertakes voyages of discovery to other worlds". This is largely true even of mental voyages. "Who hath sailed about the world of his own heart," quotes Lowell from Thomas Fuller, "sounded every creek, surveyed each corner, but that still there remains much '*terra incognita*' to himself?" It would be well if, before trying to read, we could learn how to read; before trying to study, we could learn how to study. These exercises, therefore, have in view the cultivation of one of the greatest of human faculties. They deal with simple matters because this would seem to be the best, and they aim at suggestiveness only; but if they are faithfully followed, they will result in a developed imagination and, which is particularly to the point here, an increased power of Will of the greatest value in practical life.

Continue these exercises indefinitely.

Exercise No. 8. Examine a machine of not very complex construction. Know its purpose. Understand all its parts and their mutual relations. When you have thoroughly analyzed the mechanism, close your eyes and summons it before the mind. Persist in this endeavor until you are able to form a vivid mental picture of the whole. Then mentally take it to pieces. Then mentally put the parts back together. Now try to suggest some improvement by which some of the parts may be omitted, or by which parts may be better adjusted, or by which the machine may be made to accomplish better or less expensive work. Continue this exercise with various mechanisms until you are able to see into machinery, can call up to mind its inner construction, and can with ease form mental pictures of its wholes and its parts.

Exercise No. 9. Think of some matter in your life or home or place of business where a simple device or mechanism would prove valuable by a saving of time or money. The opportunity being found, proceed to think out a suitable arrangement for the purpose. Do not become absorbed in this effort to the injury of other interests. The object here is not to make inventors, but to develop power of imagination in order that motives of Will and consequences of action may be clearly perceived. Make this exercise, therefore, a study to such end. Above all, keep a strong sense of Will thoroughly in the mind. Continue until you have acquired facility in the constructive imagination.

Exercise No. 10. Recall one of your great mistakes in life, review carefully, intensely, the various motives which appealed to you at that time. Think over their relations, their force, their persistence. Judge candidly whether you deliberated sufficiently before acting. Remember distinctly that you did not give all motives or reasons an adequate hearing. Acknowledge exactly why you yielded to some motives and rejected others. Bring all these matters before your mind with the vividness of a present experience. Then review all the consequences of your then choice. In what respect do you now see that you ought to have proceeded differently? Had you so done, what would probably have been the outcome? Suppose you were now to be put back into the former circumstances. How would you decide with present knowledge? To avoid a similar mistake in the future, you must then do what you have failed to do, namely, deliberate carefully, summons all motives into court, hear each plea, give to it all adequate consideration and weight, and vividly foresee all consequences of choice as far as possible. The present exercise is designed to assist you to these desired ends. Continue such review work until you have called up for examination all the mistakes that you can remember. Meanwhile, mightily resolve to forefend the future by giving every important matter utmost careful attention.

Exercise No. 11. Recall to memory some very attractive bit of landscape observed in your travels. Let us say it is a great piece of woods seen in autumn. Picture this scene to the soul: the undulating ground, covered with fallen leaves and dotted by occasional clumps of bushes; the many colors of the foliage still crowning the trees, whose numberless trunks lift into the canopy above and afford sunlit vistas in every direction; the play of the winds upon the gleaming leaves, fallen and drooping and still clinging; the vast quiet that broods over all, save when broken by the sighing of the breeze or the call of birds from the open; the swiftly moving stealth of squirrels along the ground or among the branches; and the strange and pleasurable moods suggested when you stood there in nature's haunt of beauty.

Now, invent reflections in connection with this scene. Proceed first, by the law of similarity. Of what does it remind you? You are to make the scene you have imagined the basis and cause of other scenes *similar* in one or more respects; and you are deliberately to analyze the suggestion, the two scenes by comparison, and the moods of thought occasioned by both, with reasons for the same. Do not fall into reverie. This is downright work. Its value depends altogether upon the amount of Will that you put into it, and the intelligence with which you control the mind during the labor involved.

Proceed, now, to make this scene the basis and cause of

another scene by *contrast.* You are to repeat the above exercise in all respects, except that contrast, and not similarity, is to furnish your material.

Follow these directions daily until their full value is apparent in imagination entirely under control of Will.

Exercise No. 12. The above directions may be repeated by substituting experience for scenery, proceeding, first, by similarity, and then by contrast. In all cases, be strongly conscious of the willing sense. Continue the exercise indefinitely.

Exercise No. 13. Read some famous poem of the imagination. It will be better to commit it to memory. Having thoroughly mastered it, by understanding every word, and by vividly picturing in the mind every element of fancy, go on to analyze it, making a clear statement in writing of its consecutive thoughts. Then, note carefully every specimen of imagination that it contains. Then, determine its faults and its beauties as a work of the imagination. Then, observe the relation and dependence of one element upon another. Then, ascertain the secret of its beauty and of its power upon thought and feeling. Learn why it has lived and exerts its acknowledged influence. What is that influence? Continue this exercise indefinitely until you have mastered many of the world's great poems.

Exercise No. 14. In a similar manner, read some famous book (not fiction), and treat its imaginative elements as secrets to be discovered and explained. Continue this work with the best in your library.

Exercise No. 15. Take a work of fiction, and give it a similar analysis. You are now dealing with pictures of life and human nature. Read so as to obtain a vivid portrait of each character. Become thoroughly acquainted with all the personages of the book. Study the reasons for their actions. Investigate their motives. Note the influence of ancestry and environment upon them. Observe whether or not they are acting in a manner that is true to life. Would you act differently? And why? Appreciate the fact that they reason falsely and do not adequately consider all reasons involved in choice, and hence, do not give due weight to the best motives that appeal to them. Go on to follow their conduct to consequences. Are these natural—demanded by previous acts and conditions? Could the characters have been improved? Or the plot? Or the general developments of the persons? Or the outcome of their actions and relations?

Make the book a piece of real life, and study it as above suggested, in order, first, that you may thoroughly understand it, and, secondly, that you may apply its lessons to your own life. Continue until you have mastered the best works of fiction in English.

In all this remember that you are cultivating the imagination for the purpose of discovering reasons for or against conduct and of appreciating consequences. By as much as you so discover and appreciate in real life must your Will become strengthened and its determination wiser.

"*The determinate exercise of the Judgment,*" says Professor W.B. Carpenter, "*which involves the comparison of ideas, can only take place under the guidance of the Will.*"

Exercise No. 16. Suppose yourself to be about to take a certain step or to perform a certain act. It is a matter of vital importance. You wish to make no mistake, for your happiness and welfare depend upon your decision. But how are you to proceed? You may choose one thing or the other. The wisdom of your choice involves the adequate consideration of two matters—motives and consequences. Apprehended consequences are motives, but this division is convenient. Under motives may be arranged reasons for and against either choice; under consequences all outcomes that you can see as likely or probably to follow your decision. If you have cultivated memory, the recollection of other similar problems that you have been compelled to solve will come to your assistance. If you have cultivated imagination, you will be enabled to see clearly the motives that appeal to you, and you will also have power to imagine yourself as entering upon one course of procedure, passing through possible consequent experiences and reaping ultimate outcomes. Here will appear the values of preceding exercises. But above all, you should bring to this imaginary problem (a real problem will serve better) a vivid sense of its reality and importance, and a feeling of strong resolution to consider it with all your might, and to solve it in the best possible manner.

Let us now suppose the problem. You are not fond of the city or town in which you are living and conducting your business. You wish to change residence and business to another place. But there are difficulties in the way. These difficulties you are now to consider.

First, recall all previous experiences in similar matters, and keep them constantly in mind. Secondly, write in brief every conceivable objection to a change. Example: from your present domicile. All your friends and associates are here. You have here a business standing of say, twenty years. Your trade or clientage is established and certain. The town is growing. Investments are fairly remunerative, and they are safe. Your property is located in this place. Taxes are rather high, but not unreasonable, and they represent improvements. Your home is good and pleasantly situated. Your family enjoy fine social relations and are fond of the town. The children are taking root. They have opportunities of value. Schools are first class. Public opinion is sound. Morals are at least average. Your age is forty-five.

On the other hand: Climate is not agreeable. Some enemies have been developed. Only a moderate business can be carried on here. Investments do not yield a large return. Taxes are increasing. The population cannot exceed a certain rather low estimate. No new railroad facilities need be expected. Manufacturing interests are not likely to become numerous. The surrounding country is agricultural, and it no longer yields its old crops. There are no mineral resources beneath the surface. The place is far removed from points of interest—the mountains, the sea, the great cities. You have long been conscious of a degree of discontent and restlessness. You believe that a new environment would stir you up to better achievements. You ought to have a larger return for your investments of time and money. You desire the advantages of a larger sphere. Your family might therein find increased opportunities for enjoyment and a start in life. You have known better society than that in which you now move.

After these imaginary presentations of reason for and against a change, a decision is still difficult. You must now go on to select tentatively some place to which you may possibly transfer your life. There may be several in mind. Each location must receive a full and careful consideration. You are lawyer and judge, and you must plead honestly as the one, and decide impartially as the other.

In each contemplated move, you must call up every possible advantage and disadvantage, especially the latter, which may be likely to accrue from any choice that you may make. After each case, for and against, has been presented, proceed carefully to weigh them as wholes, taking in the general impression of both. Now note the balance of judgment: "To go, or not to go." Then proceed to review each case, and carefully strike out all reasons that offset one another, noting, again, at the last, the general balance of judgment: "To go, or not to go." If the two general judgments disagree, set the matter aside for future consideration. If they agree, hold the matter in abeyance a time, but resolve to decide definitely after sufficient opportunity for final reflection. If then you are in doubt, stay where you are.

Proceed in a similar manner with reference to the place to which you propose to move. If after a full deliberation you are in doubt as to one place, try another. If, having determined to move, you cannot decide upon the place "to which", remain where you are. If you decide to move, stir not until the new residence has been properly determined. If that is fixed, bend every energy to move to your own advantage. When your opportunity arrives, seize it quickly. Then dismiss absolutely all regrets.

Continue these exercises indefinitely.

The Will must not only be strong; it must also act wisely. Its realest motto is:

> "I RESOLVE TO WILL—WITH POWER, AND FOR THE BEST.
> THEREFORE, ATTENTION! TO REASONS AND TO CONSEQUENCES!"

CHAPTER XXI

SOME DISEASES OF THE IMAGINATION

> *The underlying cause of all weakness and unhappiness in man, heredity and environment to the contrary notwithstanding, has always been, and is still, weak habit-of-thought. This is proven by the observed instances in which strong habit-of-thought has invariably made its masters superior to heredity, and to environment, and to illness, and to weakness of all kinds, and has redeemed them from non-success and misery, to the enjoyment of success, honor and happiness.*
>
> —Horace Fletcher

There are some dangers connected with the imagination that should be avoided, because they are enemies of a good Will. These dangers are apparent in the mental life of the majority of people, "Common sense," says James Sully in "Illusions", "knowing nothing of fine distinctions, is wont to draw a sharp line between the region of illusions and that of sane intelligence. To be the victim of an illusion is, in the popular judgment, to be excluded from the category of rational men." But "most men are sometimes liable to illusion. Hardly anybody is always consistently sober and rational in his perceptions and beliefs. A momentary fatigue of the nerves, a little mental excitement, a relaxation of the effort of attention by which we continually take our bearings with respect to the real world about us, will produce just the same kind of confusion of reality and phantasm which we observe in the insane."

It is to difficulties of this character that the present chapter seeks to turn attention, because it is believed that they are curable by good health and the resolute Will.

One of these enemies of Will is *reverie,* which is not of a true imagination because not controlled by the mind. Reverie may, therefore, be banished by the Will, and a true imagination may be made to take its place.

Regimes

Exercise No. 1. Whenever the mind exhibits a tendency to wander aimlessly from one thing to another, instantly check its roving. In order to do this, select from its pictures a single image, and deliberately proceed to elaborate that, making it vivid, building up its various elements into a complete whole. In this work, banish the reverie-mood and call up the resolute sense. Or weave the selected image into some train of purposed thought or action involving reasoning and an end to be attained. Consider the various motives and follow out the several consequences to an ultimate. Insist upon seeing vividly every picturable thing in the thought-train. Hold the mind steadily to the line determined on. Continue until the bent for reverie is displaced by a habit of definite thinking.

Some minds are troubled with various *hallucinations.* Here, again, imagination is out of control, and feelings are made real and images are rendered objective because such is the case. There are so-called invalids who would now enjoy perfect health had they not deceived themselves originally and thus brought about conditions which would ruin the health of a savage. It is not "Christian Science", but common sense, which teaches that the mind may, by resolute assertion of Will, throw off many physical discomforts. The writer once called upon a woman who had taken to her bed from sheer obstinacy. This was her only real disease. But it was real enough at that. Had she been maltreated, neglected, left to go hungry, or dragged out of her comfortable nest with the injunction to get well or get out, she would have recovered instantly.

Exercise No. 2. For a thousand imaginary ills the remedy is a thoroughly "oxidized" state of mind, a mind saturated with the atmosphere of common sense and good health, and a resolute contradiction by Will of the importance of the disease or pain. The remedy, thus, is not reiterated denial that the ill exists, for that is merely another invitation to insanity, and it often simply intensifies the difficulty; the soul should resolutely assert that the matter has no such importance as is suggested, and then proceed to forget the idea by strenuous engagement in other considerations.

Exercise No. 3. Visual and auditory hallucinations may sometimes be banished by a wise assertion of Will. The soul should intensely insist that itself is master. Conditions underlying the images or sounds should be thoroughly investigated. These may be physical, requiring rest and change of scene and diet for correction. Or they may be mental, in which case the same course may be pursued, with a complete variation of interest, this being found in matters far out of the ordinary habits of life.

Exercise No. 4. In other cases, the main thing is to get control of the hallucination. If it appears under certain conditions, compel it to appear under other conditions. Persist in substituting a different image or sound. Then compel it to vanish at will. Finally dismiss it. These directions are more easily given than followed, to be sure; but the truth is that many of our ills are due to a weak and fickle Will, and this may be strengthened and trained by wise application to the difficulties suggested.

These pages do not offer a substitute for medical treatment. They are designed merely for ills of a light and temporary form. When difficulties become more than foolishness of fickle fancy, the science of experts is called for.

Exercise No. 5. There are spirits which do not manifest to the eye, yet are terrible in power. Their arena is the heart. These are the *spirits of fear.* And these also may be banished by the resolute

Will. It is first necessary to be an *honest person.* The honest soul need fear nothing. But the honest soul is not always wise, and fears do haunt the life of such; fear of man, fear of ill-luck, fear of failure, fear of misfortune, fear of death, fear of hell, fear of God. The name of fear is legion. It is, therefore, not probable that one who has been terrorized by these devils may banish them instantly, bag and baggage, once and for all; but it is as true as life that the honest soul may in time, by the persistent Will, cast them forth forever.

You *fear men* whom you suppose to be above you. Proceed, now, to build up a perfectly honest life; then meet them at every opportunity; learn their weaknesses as well as their virtues; will incessantly to fear them no more. Remember, especially, that there are other people who, with equal foolishness, fear yourself, and that those whom you fear are very likely troubled with fears in turn for others superior in their thought to themselves. And possibly they fear you as well. It was Grant's belief that the enemy was as much afraid as himself; he would therefore strike first. If, with a politic understanding of the word "strike", you can learn to plunge into the feared atmosphere of those you fear, you will certainly in time banish this imaginary evil.

Similarly with *fear of ill luck.* This is superstition. The remedy is intelligence—as above. There are few failures with the honest soul and the persistent Will. Failure in the life of such a one is made admonition of experience and lesson for the future. *Fear of misfortune* is a coward's attitude. No misfortune ever befell an honest heart which might not be transformed into a blessing. *Fear of death* is anticipation of an experience that will or may bring its own antidote. If thou art right, fear not now, for thou wilt not then. Nature cares for the upright in that supreme hour. *Fear of hell* is either a ghost of theological making, or a most salutary and truthful incentive to climb out of hell's conditions. So long as you are out of hell now, fear nothing. If there is any danger of hell tomorrow, it is the prophecy of hell today.

It is in the power of mind to banish all irrational fears clean out of court. With a normal mind and a resolute Will, all these illusions of the imagination may be destroyed. *Cultivate the sane and resolute mood.*

"I RESOLVE TO WILL FOR MENTAL BALANCE. ATTENTION!"

PART IV

DESTRUCTION OF HABIT

CHAPTER XXII

CORRECTION OF HABITS

Impure thought, despondent, hopeless, repining, fault-finding, fretful, slanderous thought, is certain to make the blood impure and fill the system with disease.

So with certain habits of body consequent on such habits of thought, such as the habit of worry, the habit of laying undue stress on things not the most needful for the hour; the habit of trouble borrowing and many others, which permeate and influence every act of life. Their combined effect is exhaustion, and exhaustion is the real mother of most of the ills flesh is heir to.

—Prentice Mulford

"We are continually denying," said Henry Ward Beecher, "that we have habits which we have been practicing all our lives. Here is a man who has lived forty or fifty years; and a chance shot sentence or word lances him and reveals to him a trait which he has always possessed, but which, until now, he had not the remotest idea that he possessed. For forty or fifty years he has been fooling himself about a matter as plain as the nose on his face."

We now take up certain habits not regarded as immoral.

Slang

Perhaps one such unconscious habit is that of slang. Some people are, indeed, slaves to the tyrant, "Correct Style". There is a golden mean. It is related of a college professor that his usual manner of speaking was so excessively elegant that he really obscured the natural scintillations of a bright mind; he was dull where a slight admixture of the "common parlance" would have imparted vivacity to his otherwise interesting conversation. He stands as a type of the few uncanny and "literary fellows".

One may indulge slightly in slang as an agreeable concession to a work-a-day world, but its habitual use indicates a want of self-control.

"The use of *slang*," said Dr O.W. Holmes, "or cheap generic terms, as a substitute for differentiated specific expressions, is at once a sign and a cause of mental atrophy. It is the way in which a lazy adult shifts the trouble of finding any exact meaning in his (or her) conversation on the other party. If both talkers are indolent, all their talk lapses into the vague generalities of early childhood, with the disadvantage of a vulgar phraseology. It is a prevalent social vice of the time, as it has been of times that are past."

The habit may be destroyed by following the suggestions relating to profanity and garrulousness.

Remember that slang consisted originally of the "cant[8] words used by thieves, peddlers, beggars, and the vagabond classes generally."

Cultivate the society of the best speech. "If you hear poor English and read poor English," said Richard Grant White, "you will pretty surely speak poor English and write poor English."

Hesitation of Speech

It may be that the stammerer's ancestry could never get well quit of a clear statement. Many people can make no smooth

[8]Cant: insincere, esp. conventional expressions of enthusiasm for high ideals, goodness, or piety; the private language of the underworld; the phraseology peculiar to a particular class, party, profession; whining or singsong speech, esp. of beggars.

headway through a simple utterance of fact or opinion. With real "stuttering", we have here nothing to do. Those who stammer, without rhyme or reason, are but themselves at fault. Perhaps the difficulty is due to a want of "steam" sufficient to force a clear expression of thought; some people do well when excited or angry, but in calm moments, they make sad work of it. Perhaps, again, the trouble is owing to an amount of "steam" which they do not control: they speak smoothly when not disturbed, but excitement causes them to sputter like a fire-hose out of which water is failing. Persistent practise of the suggestions below ought to cure this difficulty, whatever its cause, except in case of physical deformity.

Regime 1. Recall some incident of your experience or observation occurring within the last twenty-four hours. Deliberately and rapidly recite, in an ordinary tone of voice, and as if speaking to some person, a connected account of the entire transaction. Speak as rapidly as possible. Do not permit yourself to pause an instant for want of a proper word; thrust in any word, as nearly right as may be, or even one having no related significance—any word—and go swiftly on to the end.

Regime 2. When you have begun a sentence, plunge straight through it to the close. Then proceed in the same manner with the next, and drive yourself to the finish of your account.

Regime 3. Now repeat the process, resolving to employ better language with each sentence; but do not pause an instant; force yourself to say what you desire *in some way,* no matter whether elegant or not.

Continue daily practise of these directions until your difficulty is overcome.

Regime 4. But meanwhile, one fault in your speech is this: you do not consciously think your thought in actual words. This you must learn to do. Recall, then, some subject of thought on which you have an opinion. Proceed, now, to state that opinion exactly to yourself and in an ordinary tone of voice. The exercise may be varied by pronouncing the words mentally, but do not fall into that imbecile habit of moving the lips. Your opinion must be uttered rapidly, the Will compelling the thought to march on without hesitation, no matter what an occasional word may chance to be. You have two things to learn: to think exact thoughts in actual words; and to think them with the greatest speed.

Regime 5. It will assist you, now, if you will begin to write the opinion or account as swiftly as you can dash the pen across the page. Work here also with fierce energy, never pausing an instant, but always, when tempted to hesitate, writing the best word of which you can think—or throwing in a dash or any word coming to mind. When this is done, sentence after sentence, read the whole, and proceed to criticize and correct: then rewrite in a better manner but with all possible speed.

Regime 6. Commit to memory and keep in mind the following rules:

> I will speak rapidly—or slowly, as required.
> I will never stop for a word.
> I will never pause to correct a word or a phrase.
> I will never leave a sentence unfinished.
> I will never turn back in a sentence.
> I will use the best possible language.
> I will not speak in two styles—one for common life, and one for uncommon occasions. I will adopt a good style and always employ this.
> I will not speak loosely, and I will not converse like a prig or a pedant. I will be correct, yet simple; elegant, yet unaffected.

Mind-Wandering

Elsewhere, in Chapter XVIII, will be found other pertinent remarks on this fault. The importance of the topic cannot be overestimated, and it will, therefore, bear further suggestions.

The wandering mind is the thoughtless mind. Thought loves the highway; notions climb the fences. Thoughts are trained hounds; fancies are puppies—off for every scent. It would weary the intellect of a Newton to follow the wanderings of a young dog. Wandering thoughts waste the brain and they get no "game". The uncontrolled brain is a fool's paradise. Nothing comes of the mind which cannot stick. The cure of mind-wandering is control by the Will. The practice here suggested will cure this senseless fault, and at the same time, strengthen the Will itself.

Regime 1. In reading, always proceed slowly, until you have acquired the power of rapid comprehension. Select some good sentence for reading. Read it, slowly and carefully, understanding every word of it.

Regime 2. Continue the above exercise until you can confine the mind to that thought with not the shadow of another idea. Then proceed with further reading in exactly the same way. You will not make much progress at the start. Your habit is of long standing, and it will require great patience and perseverance to destroy it. But the thing can certainly be done.

Regime 3. When about to read, ask yourself: "Why am I to read this matter?" Find that out; then insist upon getting what you are after. Read the first sentence, and ask: "What did that sentence mean and say?" Read the sentence until you know and can tell the fact or truth in your own words. Proceed thus to the close of the first paragraph, and ask: "Exactly what does this paragraph declare?" Persist in reading the same paragraph until you can relate its thought. Continue these exercises to the complete mastery of thoughtful reading. You will find your mind-wandering slowly vanishing.

Regime 4. While engaged in business or other matters, pause frequently to note what you are thinking about. You will meet with many surprises. Catch yourself indulging some train of fancy, and then ask: "Has this any value to me? Am I thinking out the matter in which I am physically engaged, or on which I set out, or am I merely running about in it like a puppy in a new field?" Keep the mind upon thoughts of value. They need not relate to death and the judgment; pleasant thoughts are not unlawful. Compel your mind to think, not only thoughts of value, but in a connected way as well. Stand guard over your own mind. Dispel every fleeting fancy and uncalled notion not germane to the thing in hand, as far as possible. Cultivate a reliable and purposeful intellect. Commit the following lines to memory, and make the verse a talisman against wandering thoughts:

> A wandering mind is like a shooting star:
> With orbit none, it yields a transient light.
> The mind God launched across Creation's bar
> Hath His omnipotence—great Reason's might

Garrulousness

The majority of people talk too much, often saying nothing, or what is perhaps, the worse for themselves, uttering words which they afterwards wish had been left unsaid. There are others who are as uncommunicative as the oyster—and not always, when they open their mouths, does a pearl fall to your prize. In social life, they are fallen logs, against which the stream of conversation dashes and from which it turns aside in sparkling agitation. In business, they are enigmas, perennial objects of suspicion. They do not, as a rule, make many friends, although when they do, these stand by to the death.

The opposite class are numerous, and, because they talk too much, are objects of a fellow-feeling among men and are believed to be amenable to improvement. The following rules will cure garrulousness, if obeyed to the letter.

Regime 1. At the beginning of each day for, say, three months, run over in your mind all matters that are of vital importance to your social and business life. You will discover some things that you ought to keep to yourself. Make an iron-clad resolution to reveal them to no human being. *Remember! Remember! Remember!* When in conversation with others, recall that resolution. *Remember! Yes, remember!* If you fail during the day, *remember! remember!* and renew the resolution on the next day. Stand by it! Carry it in mind every hour. In the evening, review your success or failure, and saturate your thought with condemnation and with fiercer determination to reform. Do not yield until you can instantly repress any impulse to speak on any subject. In three months, you will be the master of your tongue.

Regime 2. You are using too many words at all times. This fault can be corrected. You must, in order to improve, cultivate terseness of speech. Practise every day for a year the following. This is labor, but the result will amply repay you.

Regime 3. Think of a fairly long statement concerning some object, person or event. You must deliberately think in words, making an intelligible sentence. Now, write it out in full. We will call this statement "A". Repeat it, attending to your own voice. How does it sound? Is the sentence the best that you can make? If not, improve it. Now reduce it to its lowest possible terms as a clear, definite, and complete statement. Write it on another sheet of paper. Repeat it, noting its sound. Then, determine to cut it down one-third, or even by half. Persevere until this is done. Write the result on a third sheet of paper. Now, compare the three statements. Compute the per cent of reduction. You will be astonished to observe the waste of breath and language in your ordinary conversation.

Regime 4. Resolve to carry out the idea of condensation in all your speech. In the course of a few months, you will discover two things: first, your vocabulary will have become larger and better, because this effort requires the use of dictionaries and thoughtful practise with words; secondly, your manner of speaking will have become surprisingly condensed and intelligent.

Regime 5. Select, further, some author whose style is chaste and condensed. Read his works carefully, a little every day. Following the rules for memory, commit some of your author's best sentences and paragraphs. A small book that is a condensation of a larger one may be used in connection with the preceding suggestion. In time, this practice will, without any special effort on your part, greatly modify your general style of speech.

Regime 6. No one will affirm that Carlyle's tumultuous chaos of words is a finished globe of conventional economy in the matter of language; but this Thunderer has thoughts and is recognized as a wizard with our mighty English. Read the following, therefore; cut it deeply into memory, and live in the atmosphere of its suggestion:

"The great *silent* men! Looking around on the noisy inanity of the world, words with little meaning, actions with little worth, one loves to reflect on the great Empire of *Silence.* The noble, silent men, scattered here and there, each in his department; silently thinking, silently working; whom no Morning Newspaper makes mention of! They are the salt of the Earth. A country that has none or few of these is in a bad way. Like a forest which had no *roots*; which had all turned into leaves and boughs;—which must soon wither and be no forest. Woe for us if we had nothing but what we can *show* or speak. *Silence, the great Empire of* SILENCE; *higher than the stars; deeper than the Kingdoms of Death! It alone is great; all else is small.*"

Thoughtlessness

This is the habit which causes one to miss his train, forget his wife's message, send an important letter without signature, rush to keep an engagement an hour late, omit to carry his pocket-book, dress for an evening party without a necktie, leave the comb in her hair, and cry, when the house is afire: "Where is the baby?" It may and ought to be cured. The main secret of remedy is, of course, the resolute Will. Every habit which men confess can be broken, if it be thoroughly willed that the thing must and shall be done.

Regime 1. You should resolve every day until it ceases to be necessary, as soon as you rise, to remember whatever you ought to remember during that day. It would be better to so resolve at morning and at noon. At the close of the time limited, you should recall wherein you have failed, and spend a few moments in deliberate thought on the folly of this fault.

Regime 2. You should ask yourself concerning any particular matter requiring attention: "Why do I wish to remember this thing? Who will suffer if I fail? Who will be benefited if I succeed?"

Regime 3. You should make up your mind absolutely never to defer what ought to be done at some time, and may be done immediately. The moment you think of a matter that you wish to attend to, proceed instantly to do it. If it is impossible at the time, charge your mind with it again, state why it must be done, and when you will give it attention. Do it then at almost any cost. You are fixing a habit of recollection, and this is worth all inconvenience.

Regime 4. You should begin now to give your whole mind to whatever you undertake. Do nothing without full thought. Repeat to yourself: "I know what I am doing and why. This one thing I do." When the matter is finished, and before you allow yourself to think of anything else, review it carefully. Is it all complete? Is it exactly to your satisfaction? If not, go back and do it over again, following the above directions. This develops the habit of thinking on what you are doing.

Regime 5. You should never think of one thing while trying to do another—except in certain habituated tasks.

Regime 6. You should put yourself to inconvenience to make good any carelessness.

Regime 7. You should never allow yourself to become excited.

Practise daily, for three months, making a different route that you will follow in going to and returning from your place of business, and never fail.

Regime 8. Determine every day until unnecessary, to recall, at a certain exact hour, some particular matter to which you will then attend. Keep the same hour for many days; then change the hour; continue until you are the master in this respect. This will build up a habit of obeying your own orders.

Regime 9. At frequent intervals, during each day until unnecessary, stop all active work, and recall any particular matter that you ought to have attended to. Then recall any matter to which you must yet attend. Do not be hurried. Give your whole thought to these efforts. Immediately make good your negligence.

Regime 10. Never trust mere notebooks for matters which a fair memory ought to retain. Never trust anything else for dates and important business transactions. Put no confidence in mnemonics; tie no strings to your fingers; make no associations (unless of the simplest kind) as helps. Use your Will. Compel yourself to obey that power.

Indecision

There are those whose Willpower is very good when they have decided what they will do. But they find it difficult to arrive at a decision. They balance the *pros and cons* to weariness, and cannot settle the matter in hand. That is to say, they believe themselves to be engaged as indicated. The truth is, their minds are confused, and it is but vaguely that they think at all. If this is your habit—that of indecision—you must summon your entire strength to its destruction. The difficulty is more or less constitutional; nevertheless it may be overcome.

Regime 1. Carry always with you a strong sense of resolution.

Regime 2. Cultivate consciousness of self and self-possession.

Regime 3. Remember always where you are and what you are doing.

Regime 4. Under no circumstances permit yourself to become excited or confused. If you find either of these conditions obtaining, defer the matter until calmness returns. If it cannot be deferred, summons tremendous Will; remember, "I must be calm!" and decide as best you can. At the next emergency, profit by this experience. But waste no energy in useless reviews of mistakes. Store away the mood of coolness for future use.

Regime 5. Learn to think of but one thing at a time. When engaged with any matter, put the whole mind upon that alone.

Regime 6. Make the difficulty and discomfort of indecision cause for immediate resolution.

Regime 7. When in doubt, attend to motives singly. Think of one at a time clearly and forcibly. Do not become distracted by many considerations. In examining motives, force a vivid conception of each, and then of all together. Then, rapidly review all reasons, for and against, as nearly at once as possible. Then act! Decide!

Take some chances. All men must do so more or less. Waste no time with consequent regrets.

Regime 8. For at least three months resolve every morning as to how you will dress. Do this quickly. Fix the exact order of procedure. Adhere strictly to your plan. Never yield; never hesitate. Dress as rapidly as possible. Vary the order each day, as far as may be done with your combination.

Regime 9. Resolve, when you start for your office, or any objective point, that you will keep in mind what you are doing until you arrive. Do not plan the way at the start. Proceed on your way; think that you are going; at the first opportunity for varying the course, pause an instant, think of reasons for one way or another, and immediately decide—to take this car or to follow that street; at the next opportunity, repeat the process. Continue until facility in quick decision in the matter is acquired.

Regime 10. You should cultivate the habit of acting in a rapid, energetic manner. Do everything you undertake with keen thought and a strong feeling of power.

Regime 11. You should above all learn promptness. Meet every engagement on the minute. Fulfill each duty exactly on time. Never dawdle in any matter. Be decisive in all things.

Regime 12. In addition to hours and dates ordinarily fixed in your life, make many artificial resolutions relating to time and manner, and religiously carry them out to the letter. Keep forever in mind the necessity of promptness, energy, quickness of action, strength of Will.

Want of Opinion

The fundamental difficulty here is the lack of thought. People who think have opinions. Thought can be cultivated only by exercise of Will, and in three ways: by *forced efforts,* which require Will;

by *reading,* which requires intelligent comprehension, and by *observation,* which requires attention.

Regime 1. You do not observe keenly and clearly what is going on about you. You should resolve and instantly begin to *see things.* It is a great art, that of seeing correctly. The wise man is he who *sees* what other people are *merely looking at.* You should determine to see things as they are. This means that you are to find out what they are. You can begin upon any common object: the ground; the grass; household furniture. After a time, you will become interested, and you will then find yourself thinking. Then you will have opinions, because you will believe or know many matters.

Regime 2. You need to discover wherein you are ignorant. That will be comparatively easy. Then you must set about finding all that you can discover upon some particular subject. Look around; ask questions; read papers, magazines, books. Keep the end in view, to know this subject to the bottom. Do not allow yourself to be diverted from this purpose. Become a walking encyclopedia on this one thing. When you have exhausted the matter as far as possible, you will possess genuine opinions. And you will then be eager to take another subject, and will follow it to the last farthing of value. The result will be—more opinions.

Regime 3. In the meantime, you will have discovered the luxury of *intelligent* opinions, and of the habit of forming your own. People accept the opinions of others because they are aware of their own ignorance. So soon as they become themselves informed, they decline this sort of superiority. Want of opinion and want of knowledge are equivalent. The latter is the sole right remedy for the former. But there is no cure for want of brains. Without brains, the so-called opinions are fools' quips. At the brainless person Nature wrings her helpless hands. It is a finality of despair.

Opinionativeness

This habit is the outcome of a stubborn Will exercised by a blind soul. The opinionated man sees himself only. His Volitions are not so much strong and active as set and inert. The Will is here more or less diseased, because the self has no proper outlook upon life. The self supposes that it understands things, events and persons, but its real understanding is vague and partial. Could it know more, it would arrive at different views. It looks at the silver side of the shield; it ought to discover the other side; but it cannot do this. Certain aspects of events are presented; it cannot penetrate to additional phases. Views of people give it notions which are not real ideas because true motives of conduct are hidden. The opinionated person is usually wrong. As woman depends largely upon intuitions, when she betrays the fault here under consideration, it is well-nigh incurable, for intuitions are not amenable to reason. They are divine when right, but the despair of man when wrong. The difficulty here lies in the fact that the opinionated soul views all things through itself, and magnifies its own personality to enormous proportions. It is ruled by subjective conditions which shut out the relations and perspective of the world.

> Who ne'er concedes the law of truth,
> That truth transcends his mind,
> Mistakes himself for God, and, sooth,
> With open eyes—stands blind:
> His soul a world, great "views" he spawns.
> While humans laugh and Nature yawns.

Such a conception of self can only be corrected by a true realization of the personality of other people. There are those who never actually appreciate the fact that their fellows are genuine existences. To them, human beings are little more than phantoms, presenting various unsubstantial phenomena of life;

they are never *bona-fide* persons possessed of hearts and brains, and engaged in concrete realities. Why should phantoms have opinions? Themselves are real; themselves discover reasons for views; themselves are therefore entitled to opinions. This right is not universal because other minds are not by them apprehended as actual. Hence, the remedy for this species of "insanity" must go to the root of the difficulty. These people must learn to realize their fellows. If the habit of opinionativeness is to be cured, humanity must be made concrete and real in thought.

In order to do this, let the following suggestions be practised during life. After death, your happiness will largely depend upon your power to concede to your fellows a legitimate place in the universe.

Regime 1. Select one of your friends or acquaintances, and study that soul with no reference whatever to yourself. Learn his ways, his sentiments and emotions, his thoughts and motives. No matter whether these elements of his life are proper or improper, right or wrong; you are not to sit in judgment upon him, but merely to become thoroughly acquainted with his nature and character. In time, you will discover that he thinks he has various reasons for his opinions, which you are not to condemn, because that is not the thing in hand, but which you are vividly to realize as facts in his life. Above all, you will gradually find yourself thinking of him as a real being in a real body and engaged in a real life.

Regime 2. Continue this study with reference to other people about you, until you have formed the habit of feeling thoroughly the fact that you are dealing with living men and women.

Regime 3. When you have ceased to think of them as phantoms, a curious thing will occur; you will regard some of your old-time opinions as more or less confused, inadequate and baseless.

Regime 4. At all times, you should remember with whom you

are coming in contact. If your idea of human life is justifiable, you need to look upon no one as your inferior. Many people may be so, indeed, but it isn't worthwhile considering. You have, perhaps, been accustomed to deference and obedience from your employees. Such a relation demands politeness on your part for the sake of your own dignity. The person who is not polite to servants surrenders moral values. Yet politeness is merely the veneer of the Golden Rule. That rule, in all respects, should be practised toward those with whom you deal. When it governs a man's life, the "maid", the "man", the employee comes to be regarded as a human being in an exalted sense. Such an habitual regard transfers from the ranks of servants to those of fellows. You have fallen into the habit of hurling your opinions at people to whom you pay no wages because you have had the authority over those who receive the means of living at your hands. Were you to look upon your "help" as real beings, sensitive and possessed of rights, you would not arrogate to your opinions sole legality and exclusive value. Whatever you do as to "hands", you do not own the rest of mankind. It is not "good policy" to forget this trifling fact.

Regime 5. You should forever strive exactly to understand opinions opposite to your own. You cannot thrust them aside as wrong unless you know what they really are. The opinionated person seldom understands what he contradicts. A thorough knowledge of another man's thought will bring you nearer to him, and your ideas, being then compared with his, will probably not seem so huge and so unquestionably correct.

Regime 6. The study of opposite opinions involves the study of reasons. There is a possibility that, when you fully discover another person's reasons for opinions, your own reasons may undergo some alteration. It would diminish your infallibility if you could see the force with which reasons other than your own make for differing views.

Regime 7. You should occasionally recall your errors in judgment. It may be ventured with some assurance that you will be able to recollect at least one such error. If once in error, possibly many times. Burn that into your soul.

Regime 8. You should also recall the mistakes of your life. You have thus suffered injury. If you can write this on the retina of your eye, perhaps you may reform a little of your arrogant attitude. Some of your mistakes have injured others. If you do not care about this, close the present book and "gang your ain gait"[9]. The pig-pen has one remedy—fire and the sword.

Conclusion

In conclusion of the two preceding chapters, it would be well for every person occasionally to submit to self-examination as to the reign of habits, whether immoral or otherwise. Beware of the "devil's palsy of self-approbation". Let a list of personal faults be carefully and deliberately made. They should be severely scrutinized to ascertain their power and results. Then resolve to destroy them, root and branch. Begin at once. Carry the list with you. Frequently read it. Determine, again and again, to be rid of them. Give each a definite time for extirpation[10]. Preserve a record of success and failure in this respect. Read this at the close of each day of battle. Continue until free.

Meanwhile, in all things, cultivate the resolute, conquering Mood of Will. *You can be free!*

RESOLVE! "ATTENTION TO THE KING ON HIS THRONE!"

---

[9]"Gang your ain gait": A Scot's phrase meaning "Go your own way."

[10]Extirpation: to remove or destroy totally; do away with; exterminate; to pull up by or as if by the roots.

CHAPTER XXIII

CONTROL OF OTHERS

If you would work on any man, you must either know his nature and fashions, and so lead him; or his ends, and so persuade him; or his weaknesses and disadvantages, and so awe him; or those that have interest in him, and so govern him.

—Francis Bacon

The preceding directions and illustrations relate to the control of one's self. Willpower is constantly shown to embrace others as well. Here is one of the most interesting of modern subjects of inquiry.

This chapter deals with plain matters. Its subject will be treated further in the volume on "The Personal Atmosphere". There are many things in our life that are not elucidated by what some are pleased to call "Common Sense", and these will in part appear in the discussion of that work.

At the outset, we may observe certain broad principles. Without exception, these principles are possible to the large and determined Will. According to your Will-faith, so be it!

General Principles

First Principle—Belief. Genuine belief in the thing in hand makes mightily for success in the contact with others. Said Emerson: "I have heard an experienced counsellor say, that he never feared the effect upon a jury of a lawyer who does not believe in his heart that his client ought to have a verdict. If he does not believe it, his unbelief will appear to the jury, despite all his protestations, and will become their unbelief. This is that law whereby a work of art, of whatever kind, sets us in the same state of mind wherein the artist was when he made it. That which we do not believe, we cannot adequately say though we may repeat the words never so often. It was this conviction which Swedenborg expressed, when he described a group of persons in the spiritual world endeavoring in vain to articulate a proposition which they did not believe; but they could not, though they twisted and folded their lips even to indignation."

Second Principle—Confidence. A prime element in personal influence is confidence. Pizarro, the Spanish adventurer, left with one vessel and a few followers on the island of Gallo, where the greatest dangers and suffering had been endured, was offered relief by an expedition from Panama. "Drawing his sword, he traced a line with it on the sand from east to west. Then, turning towards the south, 'Friends and comrades!' he said, 'on that side are toil, hunger, nakedness, the drenching storm, desertion and death; on this side, ease and pleasure. There lies Peru with its riches; here Panama and its poverty. Choose, each man, what best becomes a brave Castilian. For my part, I go to the south.' So saying, he stepped across the line." And they followed him.

Third Principle—Enthusiasm. Enthusiasm is also a large factor in the matter. Samuel Smiles wrote very practically: "There is a contagiousness in every example of energetic conduct. The brave man is an inspiration to the weak, and compels them, as it were, to follow him. Thus Napier relates that at the combat of Vera, when the Spanish center was broken and in flight, a young officer, named Havelock, sprang forward, and, waving his hat, called upon the Spaniards to follow him. Putting spurs to his horse, he leaped the abattis[11] which protected the French front,

[11]Abattis: a line of defense consisting of a barrier of felled or live trees

and went headlong against them. The Spaniards were electrified; in a moment they dashed after him, cheering for '*El chico bianco!*' (the fair boy), and with one shock they broke through the French and sent them flying down hill."

Fourth Principle—Self-mastery. Hence the *secret of a large control of others is found in the moral mastery of self.*

It has been well written: "Keep cool, and you command everybody." An author quotes a good remark of Clarendon, who said of Hampden: "He was supreme governor over his passions, and he had thereby great power over other men's." Man may be controlled in an ignoble way by studying and ministering to his weaknesses, but a noble use of self-mastery has sublime privilege in exerting good influence over the weak spot and the foible of humanity. In either instance, the strong man is that one whose Will is steady and purposeful. Sooner or later, however, men discover their degradation in manipulated weakness, and, resenting the imposition, throw off the yoke, whenever the motive of fear ceases to restrain them.

Fifth Principle—Motives. The character of man's influence over his fellows depends upon the motives which he suggests for their action.

One may dominate multitudes by fear—Nero ruled Rome as a buffoon and a madman. Or, love may become the controlling force in personal loyalty—Jesus swayed thousands by the inspiration of His Divine goodness. In the one case influence is coercion, ceasing so soon as fear disappears, or assuming such power as to break in desperation with its own dictates; in the other case motives of fidelity are multiplied, and they become stronger as love's gracious spell continues.

---

with branches (sharpened or with barbed wire entwined) pointed toward the enemy.

Sixth Principle—Insight. The control of others demands ability to penetrate their motives and discover their plans. Of Mirabeau it was said: "It was by the same instinctive penetration that Mirabeau so easily detected the feelings of the assembly, and so often embarrassed his opponents by revealing their secret motives, and laying open that which they were most anxious to conceal. There seemed to exist no political enigma which he could not solve. He came at once to the most intimate secrets, and his sagacity alone was of more use to him than a multitude of spies in the enemy's camp. …He detected in a moment every shade of character; and, to express the result of his observations, he had invented a language scarcely intelligible to anyone but himself; had terms to indicate fractions of talents, qualities, virtues, or vices—halves and quarters—and, at a glance, he could perceive every real or apparent contradiction. No form of vanity, disguised ambition, or tortuous proceedings could escape his penetration; but he could also perceive good qualities, and no man had a higher esteem for energetic and virtuous characters." *This ability may be successfully cultivated.*

Seventh Principle—Cooperation. Permanent influence over others flows from the enlistment of their strength. The supremest individual power in this respect is gauged by the pleasure which it offers as inducement to surrender, or by the sense of right to which appeal is made for alliance, or by suggestion of highest self-interest as a reason for loyalty. The best rule in the control of others is the Golden Rule. In the long run, life reciprocates with those who do unto others as they would that others should do unto them. That power of Will which can compel one to be polite, considerate, patient, helpful, luminously cheerful, is sure to cast a large and agreeable spell upon our fellows.

It is not to be understood that these suggestions seek to put a premium upon what is called "policy". Men are not all selfishness. There is a divine reason in humanity which makes it amenable to the kingly sway of sincerity, reality and righteousness. The native vigor of downright honesty creates a current of attraction that is hard to resist. The people put faith in Grant, because, no doubt, of manifest ability, but also for the reason that they saw in the silent commander an actual man. When a soul succeeds in convincing others that it is genuinely possessed by an eternal truth or principle, the Infinite steps in and accords him a public coronation as the leader. Saul among the Jews was simply fantastic; David was a real argument for a king and a throne. Stephen A. Douglas, with culture and political machinery behind him, was no match for Lincoln, because in this man burned the unquenchable fires which blazed in the heart of the North. It was the "Little Giant" against "Honest Old Abe" and the great slavery-hating States. Here the Will, that years before had shaken its clenched fist at the "Institution", rose to grandeur and assumed the robes of prophet and deliverer.

Eighth Principle—Willpower. The resolute Will is leader by Nature's choice. If itself is throned in righteousness, its sway is certain and permanent—in a modified sense at times, to be sure, but not infrequently with limits outlasting the span of its possessor's life. Cromwell's Will made him "Ironsides". William of Orange competed with the subtlety, patience and tireless pertinacity of Philip the Second, and won a lasting influence that the Spanish king could not destroy by power of wealth, position or ecclesiastical backing. These historic dramas are huge representations of smaller affairs in every community. In the fullest sense, *a strong Will for control of others is a right Will.*

Suggestions

The great subject of personal magnetism is elaborately and practically set forth in the author's work, "Power for Success", to which the student is referred.

If you will make the following suggestions a part of your working capital, you are on the highway of agreeable and satisfactory relations with your fellows. Though the matter seems simple enough in theory, it will tax your perseverance to the utmost to carry it out to practical results:

1. Never show temper.
2. Never betray envy or jealousy.
3. Indulge in no sarcasms.
4. Keep unpleasant opinions to yourself.
5. Tell no man an uncomfortable truth, if this can with honesty be avoided, and make sure that you disclose the motive of a well-wisher, if you must utter the facts.
6. Make no remark about others that you would not instantly make in their presence.
7. Make no remark about others that you must know will, if instantly reported to them, cause enmity against you or injure their interests.
8. Never criticize to a man his wife, to a wife her husband, to a parent the child, to the child its parent, nor to any person a relative or friend.
9. When conversing with others make sure with whom you are talking in these respects, and in regard to all social, business, political, and religious matters.
10. Never make a joke that hurts anyone present or absent.
11. Never relate anything that might not with propriety be repeated to a lady just introduced to you.
12. Make no promise without knowing that you can fulfill it. Then fail not.
13. Make your word good promptly. If you cannot, explain to the person involved.
14. Never dodge a creditor.
15. Don't be a bore.
16. Ride your hobby in the backyard.
17. Permit other people to have views.
18. See things as they are; tell them as you see them—when good sense and kindness allow.

19. Put a heart into your handshake.
20. Be as courteous to "low" as to "high".
21. Be considerate of the rights and feelings of others. How about your barking dog? Your thrumming piano? Your lusty boy?
22. Carry the Golden Rule on your sleeve.
23. Never rub a man the wrong way.
24. Never contradict an irritated person.
25. Never get into an argument in a parlor nor on the street.
26. Never ridicule a man's pet theory nor a woman's foible.
27. Never ridicule a person's walk, dress, habit, or speech.
28. Never laugh at weakness.
29. Permit yourself to sneer at nothing. The sneer is the devil's laugh.
30. Never hold anyone in contempt. At least conceal the feeling like a death's-head.
31. Never order people about.
32. Be absolutely honest everywhere.
33. Be gracious and accommodating.
34. Cultivate generosity of pocket and of thought.
35. On sixty dollars a month don't browbeat the people. You are only a ticket-agent, a steamboat purser, a hotel clerk, a bank teller. Not much, after all, if you are to treat the public as though you were a lord. A good deal if you are decent.
36. Don't stalk along the street as though you were superfine, angelic, distilled wonder of imperial blueblood. You are exceedingly lovely, to be sure; yet just a woman—bones, fat, blood, nerves, weaknesses and blunders—like the rest of womankind.
37. Never antagonize others unless principle demands it. And then, hold the purpose in view, "To win, not to alienate".
38. Never pass judgment upon others without first mentally "putting yourself in his place".

39. Never utter that judgment unless you are convinced that this will accomplish some good or satisfy the reasonable demands of a definite principle.
40. Never permit your general opinion of a person to blind you to his good qualities.
41. In discussions, never interrupt, a speaker, nor talk in a loud tone of voice. If you cannot speak without interruption, go away, or keep silence. One who will not hear your views is not worth the trouble of excited conversation.
42. Preface all statement of difference of opinion with a conciliatory word.
43. Never insist upon doing business with a person who evidently does not wish to see you—unless you are a policeman, a sheriff, a tax-collector, a lawyer's clerk, a physician or a messenger of death.
44. If your man is busy, yet makes an effort to be polite, get out of his presence as quickly and pleasantly as possible. Go again when he feels better.
45. Don't try to do business with a madman.
46. Don't try to conciliate a pig; it is always best to let him alone.
47. Don't sell a man what he doesn't want.
48. Don't sell a man an inferior article which he believes to be a superior.
49. Don't ask a favor from a person whom you haven't treated properly.
50. Don't try to fool people whose business it is to know people.
51. Always grant a favor if reasonably possible.
52. Don't try to down a man who knows more about a subject than you do.
53. Don't criticize or condemn matters into which you have never delved to discover merits or demerits. How can

you say whether it is right or wrong when you don't know its real or pretended principles?

54. Bear in mind that a friend is always worth more than an enemy. "Grudges" and ill feelings toward other men wreck havoc in the brain substance.
55. Be above petty jealousies, or a continual fretting about what somebody said or did.
56. Cultivate the ability, in dealing with others, to turn aside cutting remarks, either real or fancied. Don't have super-sensitive feelings that are cut by every zephyr of jest.
57. Remember Carlyle's "great silent men"—don't tell everything you know, either concerning others or relating to your own affairs.
58. Don't tell things "before they are ripe".
59. Don't launch a project until you have looked on every possible side of it. Sometimes the unobserved side is the one where the cave-in starts.
60. Always use pleasant words; this is not expensive, and you know not when the boomerang may return. A bad word is like a mule's hind feet; it will wait years for its one chance—and it usually gets that chance.
61. Treat every man, woman and child as though you were just about to confer a great favor—but avoid all condescension.
62. Make sure that your way is best before insisting upon it. Defer such insisting until you have won over the other person.

CHAPTER XXIV

Conclusion: The Symmetrical Existence

Our labors are now nearly concluded. Henceforth it only remains to carry out in daily life the ideas of the preceding pages. The book is not a treatise; it seeks to be a teacher, and thus leaves much to the intelligence of the reader. If it proves suggestive and leads to practical efforts for culture of the Will, the devotion of the long period required for its mastery will surely be justified.

As M. Guizot said to his class in lecturing on the "History of Civilization":

"The good fortune to have all the faculties called into action, so as to ensure a full and free development of the various powers both of mind and body, is an advantage not too dearly paid for by the labor and pain with which it is attended."

It is hoped that the following are among the *results achieved:*

The fundamentals of the mental constitution have been more fully disclosed.

The reader has been introduced to his own center of power, the Will, and has perceived some of the tests and secrets of success in life.

A neglected fact has been made plain, that the Will may be cured when defective, and thus trained and developed.

Recognition of the reader's self has been aroused—as a psychic power possessed of two psychic instruments, the body and the mind.

Certain more specific results follow these considerations:

First. The body and the senses are better understood and controlled.

Life demands clear *soul-windows.*

Correct *hearing* allies with genius.

In the sense of *smell*, the chemistry of instinct prepares for intelligent mastery.

The sense of *taste* foreruns the discriminations of a purposeful art.

The sense of *touch* advance-guards the soul's progress.

The *nervous* values of existence are measured by the degree of restraint imposed upon the nerve-system.

The *hands* should be the great art-servants of the mind.

Nerves and muscles act rightly together as they are mastered by *determined intelligence.*

The Will enjoins *health*; and its power depends upon the amount of order obtaining within its kingdom.

The labor which involves these discoveries originates indomitable *Willpower.*

Second. The mind has become a new kingdom, surveyed and given government.

The mind that can master *attention,* achieves.

The gift of *reading* depends for value upon the focusing Will.

The attribute of *thought* is kingly according to the degree of concentrated, personality behind it.

Masterful personality anticipates the future as its *memory* realizes the past.

The pioneer of life, which is the *imagination,* makes or destroys by as much as personality has willed *moral* or immoral *purpose.*

Willed moral purpose has the absolute power over all *habituated action.*

Man's *relations with his fellows* is rightly masterful if the reasonable Will is dominant.

The ability to *converse with the voiceless crowd,* any ordinary audience, is not a gift nor a trick, but is an extension of usual communication by the magnetic personality laboriously acquired.

The subtle secret of *true magnetism* is a mighty Will morally determined.

The *Personal Atmosphere* is a vibrant center to be given moral quality by high-purposed Will.

The *child* may become the supreme benefactor of the man.

The labor which involves these discoveries originates self-conscious and indomitable *power of Will.*

Third. A deathless interest in such and further important discoveries appears.

Interest awakened in self—hitherto largely unknown.

A wonderful domain has opened, causing astonishment that it should have been so long neglected.

Do educated people know themselves? Literature and schools abundant! Meanwhile, the psychic self pores and bores, unmindful and uninstructed that it is psychic or has a power of Will, and that this is given to be grown, and nurtured, and trained for ultimate destiny.

For, observe!

Nowhere, today, probably, exists a college or university wherein the individual shall study and master himself to a degree, before engaging in the smaller conquest of infinite worlds.

But what history so valuable as that of a man's own growing soul?

What science so imperative as that of a man's own bones, nerves, muscles, limbs, organs, senses, functions?

What psychology so important to know as your own?

What power so needful to understand as the electric nerve-force, the secreting and expanding dynamics of thought, the sovereign energy of Will?

Discovery of the value of systematic labor in the fundamental fields of self for its own improvement.

Is it not largely true that prevailing educational methods set minds at work upon tasks concerning ten thousand matters, more or less remotely related to the growth of the mind, rather than upon matters in the mind directly related to these multitudinous facts, so-called?

It is like trying to improve a machine by working it on inconceivable miscellanies of tasks, when reason would suggest the definite understanding and improvement of the mechanism preparatory to its adapted work.

Man's education should first concern his own fundamental powers and possibilities.

This requires more than one regime with every department of his constitution.

The value, therefore, of systematic labor on as well as with the senses and the various mental powers cannot be overestimated.

This value should be directly and deliberately sought—in the man's self, not merely in an universe, the worth of which, to him, depends wholly upon what he knows and masters of himself.

The universe, as a field of endeavor, reacts upon the individual, to be sure. But the true goal is to get the man to react rightly upon the universe. This requires self-development, sought by direct methods, as well as by the roundabout methods of objective analysis and attack.

The direct and conscious development of Will, understood as within, as the man's master or his servant, as his maker or his destroyer.

If this book has been worked into the student, he has emerged from its pages a joyous, conquering Will, a masterful personality. He ought now to decide with the prompt and compelling power of a rifle-shot. He ought now to "brake his wheels" with divine authority. He ought now to persist and sleuth-hound his purposes with the tenacity of nature's laws.

He will not have transcended his original endowments, but his true possibilities will certainly have come to the fore. That is his whole measure of responsibility and success.

If he has become self-reliant—a man who can stand alone or go alone, as his real interest may demand, he has achieved the

Mood of the gods, confidence in his own throne and dominion.

The book has undoubtedly suggested many possible exercises not found in its pages. This is a value; it implies power in the reader. All such suggestions should be tried, tested, and, if practicable and useful, adopted, for temporary purposes or for permanent regime.

Some additional chapters might have been written, as, for example, on the relation of the Will to knowledge, the place of Will in belief, the Will and the beautiful. But such chapters would prove afield of the end in view—a great Will. All exercises given tend to this end. Only in a secondary manner, probably, would practice in willing for belief or the cultivation of taste have so resulted.

It is a commonplace, however, that knowledge, in itself and as to its kind, demands willed purpose and willed selection; that right beliefs are legitimately within the province of a healthy and determined Will, in the way of forcing honest investigation and true methods, etc.; and that intelligent Will has much to do with the appropriation of art and the beautiful in general.

You exist to help. This requires that you seek to know what the nature of things has designed for you. This is your goal—none other—your life, your immortality.

Said Wilhelm von Humboldt: "The end of man, or that which is prescribed by the eternal or immutable dictates of reason, and not suggested by vague and transient desires, is the highest and most harmonious development of his powers to a complete and consistent whole; the object towards which every human being must ceaselessly direct his efforts, and on which especially those who design to influence their fellowmen must ever keep their eyes, is the individuality of power and development."

John Stuart Mill, in comment, said: "Human nature is not a machine to be built after a model, and set to do exactly the work prescribed for it, but a tree, which requires to grow and develop itself on all sides, according to the tendency of the inward forces which make it a living thing."

And now, in all our work, it is best to remember that life is not a judgment to drudgery. It is a glory, a dignity, an opportunity, a prelude and a reward. The true life has deep content—

In itself,
In its worlds,
In its brotherhood,
In its death-swallowing hope.

And it is for the body to rest, as well as to toil.

And it is for the mind to relax and change, as well as to concentrate.

And it is for the man to play, to rejoice with the hills, to throb with the sea, to laugh with nature, as well as to struggle and pile up victories.

But it is for the Will to slumber not, to relax never, to go forth day and night, in the full majesty of conquest.

For, to this end came the King to his Throne.

Lightning Source UK Ltd.
Milton Keynes UK
UKHW022055110123
415160UK00012B/1820